1971

The Age of Dickens spans the period from 1836, when *The Pickwick Papers* first appeared, to the novelist's death in 1870. These were years of great progress, during which Britain reaped the rewards of the Industrial Revolution and established herself as 'the workshop of the World'. It was also a time when poverty, bad housing, illiteracy and disease were widespread.

The popularity which Charles Dickens enjoyed during his lifetime stemmed from his skill as a story-teller. To those who lived during the middle years of the nineteenth century, characters like Sam Weller, Mr Micawber, Fagin, Scrooge, Mrs Gamp, eccentric though they often were, seemed as real as the folks next door. But Dickens was more than a teller of tales. He was also a social reformer, who cared deeply about the human misery which he saw around him.

What was Britain like at the time when Dickens was writing such masterpieces as *David Copperfield* and *Oliver Twist*? His own works can supply part of the answer, for he was a keen observer of people and places. Other contemporary sources have been used; these include edited extracts from parliamentary debates, government reports, speeches, diaries, letters, newspapers, novels, pamphlets, poems, songs, etc.

Illustrated throughout with pictures drawn from contemporary sources, this addition to the PUTNAM DOCUMENTARY HISTORY SERIES offers an exciting and authentic approach to history studies.

B

The Age of Dickens

by Patrick Rooke

G. P. PUTNAM'S SONS – NEW YORK

THE PUTNAM DOCUMENTARY HISTORY SERIES

Contents

The Illustrations

1 The England of 'Boz'

CHARLES DICKENS, one of England's greatest novelists, was born at Portsmouth of middle-class parents. His mother, a gentle, warm-hearted person, was kept busy looking after a large, young family; between 1810 and 1823 she had seven children, two of whom died in infancy. Nevertheless she found time to teach Charles to read and write and he was soon devouring *Robinson Crusoe, Don Quixote, The Arabian Nights* and any other book on which he could lay his hands. His father was employed as a clerk by the Navy Pay Department. Though loved by his family, this cheerful man had a serious weakness: he always spent more money than he earned. This led him into debt and twice resulted in his imprisonment. Some years later Charles Dickens was to portray his father as Mr Micawber in *David Copperfield*, a book which tells us more about the writer's life than any of his other works. *Charles Dickens (1812–70)*

Mounting debts threatened the family in 1823 when they were living in London. Charles's mother tried to make some money by opening a school, Mrs Dickens' Establishment for Young Ladies, but it was one of the biggest flops in history. Not a single pupil enrolled. The following year her husband was arrested and sent to Marshalsea Prison. Mr Micawber could well be Mr Dickens:

' "Mr Micawber's difficulties are almost overwhelming just at present," said Mrs Micawber; "and whether it is possible to bring him through them I don't know ..." Poor Mrs Micawber! She said she had tried to exert herself; and so I have no doubt, she had. The centre of the street door was perfectly covered with a great brass plate, on which was engraved "Mrs Micawber's Boarding Establishment for Young Ladies": but I never found that any young lady *'David Copperfield'*

Facing page Charles Dickens in 1868, two years before his death

had ever been to the school there; or that any young lady ever came, or proposed to come; or that the least preparation was ever made to receive any young lady. The only visitors I ever saw or heard of, were creditors. *They* used to come at all hours, and some of them were quite ferocious ... At these times Mr Micawber would be transported with grief and mortification, even to the length (as I was once made aware by a scream from his wife) of making motions at himself with a razor; but within half an hour afterwards, he would polish up his shoes with extraordinary pains, and go out, humming a tune with a greater air of gentility than ever (1).'

Marshalsea
Prison
Marshalsea Prison itself was a grim and forbidding building, as Dickens once described: 'Thirty years ago there stood, a few doors short of the church of Saint George, in the borough of Southwark, on the left-hand side of the way going southward, the Marshalsea Prison. It had stood there many years before, and it remained there some years afterwards; but it is gone now, and the world is none the worse without it.

'It was an oblong pile of barrack building, partitioned into squalid houses standing back to back, so that there were no back rooms; environed by a narrow paved yard, hemmed in by high walls duly spiked at top (2).'

Dickens
starts
work
Charles suffered from the family's financial difficulties. First, his precious books were sold. Then, on his twelfth birthday, he started work at Warren's Blacking Factory, an old, rat-infested building by the Thames. His pay was six shillings a week. Something of the bitterness which he felt was later recorded in *David Copperfield*, though the young hero of this book is employed by a bottling firm:

'Murdstone and Grinby's trade was among a good many kinds of people, but an important branch of it was the supply of wines and spirits to certain packet-ships. I forget now where they chiefly went ... I know that a great many empty bottles were one of the consequences of this traffic, and that certain men and boys were employed to examine them against the light, and reject those that were flawed, and to rinse and wash them. When the empty bottles ran short, there were labels to be pasted on full ones, or corks to be fitted to them, or seals to be put upon the corks, or finished bottles to be packed in casks. All this work was my work, and of the boys employed upon it I was one ...

'No words can express the secret agony of my soul as I sank into this companionship; compared these henceforth everyday associates with those of my happier childhood—not to say with Steerforth, Traddles, and the rest of those boys; and felt my hopes of growing up to be a learned and distinguished man crushed in my bosom. The deep remembrance of the sense I had, of being utterly without hope now; of the shame I felt in my position; of the misery it was to my young heart to believe that day by day what I had learned, and thought, and delighted in, and raised my fancy and my emulation up by, would pass away from me, little by little, never to be brought back any more; cannot be written (3).'

In April 1824 Mr Dickens inherited a sum of money which paid off his debts. Charles was now able to leave the hated blacking factory and went to Wellington House Academy, where he stayed for two years.

Dickens as reporter

When he left school he became an office boy to a firm of solicitors. But this did not satisfy him. His ambition was to become a Parliamentary reporter and in his spare time he began to learn shorthand. By 1832 his new career was underway and he was present in the House of Commons while the Reform Bill was being hotly debated. It was an historic occasion. This is one of the Bill's resolutions:

'It is expedient to take effectual measures for correcting divers abuses that have long prevailed in the choice of members to serve in the commons house of parliament, to deprive many inconsiderable places of the right of returning members, to grant such privilege to large, populous and wealthy towns, to increase the franchise of the knights of the shire, to extend the electors' franchise to many of His Majesty's subjects who have not heretofore enjoyed the same, and to diminish the expense of elections (4).'

The Reform Act of 1832 disappointed many of its supporters. Only a small minority of the population was still allowed to vote. There was no secret ballot at elections and bribery, such as 'election dinners', was commonplace.

Politicians

As a reporter Dickens was shocked by what he saw of the way that government was run. His disgust is reflected in the politicians who appear in his novels. An official report showed that Dickens did not exaggerate:

'With regard to the city of Hereford, can you state any circumstances connected with bribery at elections?—I believe bribery to have existed at Hereford.

'Since the passing of the Reform Bill?—Yes, and to a much more considerable extent than before (5).'

Dickens portrayed these abuses in *Pickwick Papers* (1837): 'The speeches of the two candidates, though differing in every other respect, afforded a beautiful tribute to the merit and high worth of the electors ... Both said that the trade, the manufactures, the commerce, the prosperity of Eatanswill, would even be dearer to their hearts than any earthly object; and each had it in his power to state that he was the man who would eventually be returned.

'There was a show of hands; the Mayor decided in favour of the Honourable Samuel Slumkey, of Slumkey Hall. Horatio Fizkin, Esquire, of Fizkin Lodge, demanded a poll and a poll was fixed accordingly ...

'During the whole time of the polling, the town was in a perpetual fever of excitement. Everything was conducted on the most liberal and delightful scale. Exciseable articles were remarkably cheap at all the public houses ... A small body of voters remained unpolled at the very last. They were calculating and reflecting persons, who had not yet been convinced by the arguments of either party, although they had frequent conferences with each. One hour before the close of the poll, Mr Perker solicited the honour of a private interview with these intelligent, these noble, these patriotic men. It was granted. His arguments were brief but satisfactory. They went in a body to the poll; and when they were returned, the Honourable Samuel Slumkey, of Slumkey Hall, was returned also (6).'

Dickens did not think much of the average politician: '[Mr Gregsbury] was a tough, burly, thick-headed gentleman, with a loud voice, a pompous manner, a tolerable command of sentences with no meaning in them, and in short of every requisite for a very good member indeed (7).'

'The best club in London'

To Dickens, Parliament was in disrepute: 'Britannia, sitting meditating one fine day (perhaps in the attitude in which she is presented on the copper coinage) discovers all of a sudden that she wants Mr Veneering in Parliament. It occurs to her that Veneering is a "representative man" and that Her Majesty's faithful Commons

Holborn, a crowded thoroughfare in Dickens' London

are incomplete without him, so, Britannia mentions to a legal
gentleman of her acquaintance that if Veneering will "put down"
£5,000, he may write a couple of initial letters after his name at
the extremely cheap rate of £2,500 per letter ...'

'"But you have not imported to me," remarks Veneering, "what
you think of my entering the House of Commons?"'

'"I think," rejoins Twemlow, feelingly, "that it is the best club
in London" (8).'

Between 1800 and the passing of the 1832 Reform Act the *London*
population of London soared from 865,000 to one and a half
million. This rapid growth produced many problems. Serious over-
crowding was one. The narrow noisy streets could hardly cope
with the increased traffic of horses, coaches and carts. Sanitary
conditions were poor; the Thames was a 'filthy river' and the
Serpentine, in Hyde Park, little better than an open sewer. Even
wealthy districts like Belgravia and Westminster were unpaved and
plagued by foul smells which most people—even the rich—were
resigned to.

13

As a child Dickens explored London and the fascination that he then felt for this booming city remained with him throughout his life: 'When I was a very small boy indeed, both in years and stature, I got lost one day in the City of London ... I wandered about ... staring at the British merchants, and inspired by a mighty faith in the marvellousness of everything. Up courts and down courts— in and out of yards and little squares—peeping into counting-house passages and running away—poorly feeding the echoes in the court of the South Sea House with my timid steps—roaming into Austin Friars, and wondering how the Friars used to like it—ever staring at the British merchants, and never tired of the shops—I rambled on, all through the day (9).'

In *Sketches by Boz* (1836) he remembered the maze of London's alleys: 'We will make for Drury Lane, through the narrow streets and dirty courts which divide it from Oxford Street, and that classical spot adjoining the brewery at the bottom of Tottenham Court Road, best known to the initiated as the "Rookery" (10).'

People in Dickens's day had little idea of public health: 'The *Filth and* filthy and miserable appearance of this part of London can hardly *poverty* be imagined by those (and there are many such) who have not witnessed it. Wretched houses with broken windows patched with rags and paper: every room let out to a different family, and in many instances to two or even three—fruit and "sweet-stuff" manufacturers in the cellars, barbers and red-herring vendors in the front parlours, cobblers in the back; a bird-fancier on the first floor, three families on the second, starvation in the attics, Irishmen in the passage, a "musician" in the front kitchen, and a char-woman and five hungry children in the back one—filth everywhere —a gutter before the houses and a drain behind—clothes drying and slops emptying, from the windows; girls of fourteen or fifteen, with matted hair, walking about barefoot, and in white greatcoats, almost their only covering; boys of all ages, in coats of all sizes and no coats at all; men and women, in every variety of scanty and dirty apparel, lounging, scolding, drinking, smoking, squabbling, fighting, and swearing (11).'

On Easter Monday each year, the populace struggled and fought their way out for a day's holiday in the peaceful fields of Green-wich, south of the Thames: 'The road to Greenwich during the

15

Facing page The Little Sanctuary. Poor areas like this were the source for much of Dickens' writings

whole of Easter Monday is in a state of perpetual bustle and noise. Cabs, hackney-coaches, "shay" carts, coal-wagons, stages, omnibuses, sociables, gigs, donkey-chaises—all crammed with people (for the question never is, what the horse can draw, but what the vehicle will hold), roll along at their utmost speed; the dust flies in clouds (11).'

'The Pickwick Papers' London was for Dickens a rich source of ideas for his early stories and sketches. At first these pieces appeared anonymously, then under the pseudonym of Boz. It was the publication of *The Pickwick Papers* in monthly parts from March 1836 to November 1837, however, which established his reputation as a writer. Within a short time Pickwick and Samuel Weller were loved and talked of throughout England, and so was the name of their creator.

The writer, G. K. Chesterton, once wrote: 'Pickwick will always be remembered as the great example of everything that made Dickens great; of the solemn conviviality of great friendships, of the erratic adventures of old English roads, of the hospitality of old English inns, of the great fundamental kindliness and honour of old English manners. First of all, however, it will always be remembered for its laughter, or, if you will, for its folly. A good joke is the one ultimate and sacred thing which cannot be criticised (12).'

Pickwick Club The famous Pickwick Club was a 'corresponding society', as its minutes recorded: 'That the Corresponding Society of the Pickwick Club is therefore hereby constituted; and that Samuel Pickwick, Esq., GCMPC, Tracy Tupman, Esq., MPC, Augustus Snodgrass, Esq., MPC, and Nathaniel Winkle, Esq., MPC, are hereby nominated and appointed members of the same; and that they be requested to forward, from time to time, authenticated accounts of their journeys and investigations ... to the Pickwick Club, stationed in London (13).'

This extract from *The Pickwick Papers*, which chronicled the famous meeting between Mr Pickwick and Sam Weller, affords a fascinating glimpse into social intercourse in Dickens's day:

'"There is a man in the passage now," said Mr Tupman.

"It's the man I spoke to you about," said Mr Pickwick. "I sent for him up to the Borough this morning. Have the goodness to call him up, Snodgrass." Mr Snodgrass did as he was desired; and Mr

Samuel Weller forthwith presented himself ...

"Now with regard to the matter on which I, with the con-
currence of these gentlemen, sent for you," said Mr Pickwick.

"That's the pint, sir," interposed Sam; "out with it, as the father said to the child, wen he swallowed a farden."

"We want to know in the first place," said Mr Pickwick, "whether you have any reason to be discontented with your present situation."

"Afore I answers that 'ere question, gen'l'm'n," replied Mr Weller, "*I* should like to know, in the first place, whether you're a goin' to purwide me with a better?"

A sunbeam of placid benevolence played on Mr Pickwick's features as he said, "I have half made up my mind to engage you myself."

"Have you, though?" said Sam. Mr Pickwick nodded in the affirmative.

"Wages?" inquired Sam.

"Twelve pounds a year," replied Mr Pickwick.

"Clothes?"

"Two suits."

"Work?"

"To attend upon me; and travel about with me and these gentlemen here."

"Take the bill down," said Sam, emphatically. "I'm let to a single gentleman, and the terms is agreed upon."

"You accept the situation?" inquired Mr Pickwick.

"Cert'nly," replied Sam. "If the clothes fits me half as well as the place, they'll do." (14)'

But the rural England of Pickwick, with its old roads and coaching inns, was fast disappearing. Great changes lay ahead in the middle years of the century—years which may well be called the Age of Dickens.

In June 1837 Victoria became Queen. She was only eighteen.
The previous year this slender young girl had met her German cousin Prince Albert and a marriage between the two seemed likely. Much to Albert's dismay, however, the excitement of ascending the throne made Victoria forget such plans. He wrote plaintively to his old tutor: 'Victoria is said to be incredibly stubborn ... she delights in court ceremonies, etiquette and trivial

formalities. These are gloomy prospects ... She is said not to take the slightest interest in Nature, to enjoy sitting up at night and sleeping late into the day (15).'

Prince Albert But the pair did become engaged, in October 1839, and they were happily married the following February: 'I am writing to you today on one of the happiest days of my life to send you the most joyful possible news. Yesterday in a private audience V. declared her love for me, and offered me her hand, which I seized in both mine

Left Queen Victoria and *right* Prince Albert, her Consort

and pressed tenderly to my lips. She is so good and kind to me that I can scarcely believe such affection should be mine (16).'

Victoria's uncles and predecessors, George IV and William IV, had not endeared themselves to the English people, and the throne had been brought into disrepute. The young Queen and her German Consort now had to face much criticism. Amongst the satire which poured out was a song entitled, *The German Bridegroom*, by 'the Honourable J.W.':

> He comes the bridegroom of Victoria's choice,
> The nominee of Lehzen's* vulgar voice;
> He comes to take 'for better or for worse'
> England's fat Queen and England's fatter purse.

Punch (1843) commented drily on Queen Victoria's theatre-going: 'The Opera-house, on the occasion of her Majesty's state visit, was not nearly so full as Drury Lane had been, a little while before, on a similar occasion. This is very easily accounted for. The Queen at Drury Lane was a novelty indeed, but the Queen at the Opera is almost an everyday occurrence.'

In the same year, *Punch* noted Prince Albert's rise in status at the time of prorogation of Parliament: 'It will be seen that Prince Albert, who formerly upon state occasions sat on a little chair, has had a large one made for him. At the last prorogation, he was allowed a moderate-sized seat; but now he is favoured with one in every respect the same as that prepared for her Majesty. What has Prince Albert lately done to entitle him to a larger share of elbow-room than was formerly allowed? The Prince has evidently been "looking up" ever since his marriage. On his first taking part in state ceremonies, he used to sit upon footstools, hassocks, or anything he could get; but he was soon promoted; and we find him at one of the *levées* of last year suddenly elevated to a music-stool.'

Criticism of the monarchy continued unabated: 'As going abroad is generally considered to "finish the education", we may presume that something has been added by her foreign trip to that perfection which it was always customary to find in Queen Victoria. A trip to the Continent, which is supposed to give polish to the lawyer's clerk, and add brilliancy to the bagman, must have rendered her Majesty—dazzling as she was before—something almost too bright to contemplate (17).'

Value of foreign travel

It was to be many years before Victoria really won the hearts of her subjects.

* Baroness Lehzen was Lady Attendant to Victoria.

2 The Hungry Forties

BENJAMIN DISRAELI, who was later to become prime minister of Britain, wrote a novel in 1845 called *Sybil*; the book was published with the alternative title of *The Two Nations*. In Disraeli's view, the people of England did not form one nation, but two—the rich and the poor. Here is Disraeli's portrait of a pauper child:

'Such was the nameless one of whom we speak. We cannot say he thrived; but he would not die. So, at two years of age, his mother being lost sight of, and the weekly payment having ceased, he was sent out in the street to "play", in order to be run over. Even this expedient failed ... They gave him no food: he foraged for himself, and shared with the dogs the garbage of the streets. But he still lived; stunted and pale, he defied even the fatal fever which was the only habitant of his cellar that never quitted it (18).'

Indifference to poverty by the rich is satirised by Dickens in strong words like these: '[Mr Bounderby] was a rich man: banker, merchant, manufacturer, and what not. A big, loud man, with a stare, and a metallic laugh. A man made out of a coarse material, which seemed to have stretched to make so much of him. A man with a great puffed head and forehead, swelled veins in his temples, and such a strained skin to his face that it seemed to hold his eyes open, and lift his eyebrows up. A man with a pervading appearance on him of being inflated like a balloon, and ready to start. A man who could never sufficiently vaunt himself a self-made man. A man who was always proclaiming, through that brassy speaking-trumpet of his, his old ignorance and poverty. A man who was the Bully of humility (19).'

Facing page Disraeli, like Dickens, realised the need for social reforms

Struggling craftsmen, many of them new to urban life, marvelled at the prosperity of the new race of industrialists. In her novel *Mary Barton* (1848), famous as a social document, Mrs Gaskell wrote: 'At all times it is a bewildering thing to the poor weaver to see his employer removing from house to house, each one grander than the last, till he ends in building one more magnificent than all, or withdraws his money from the concern, or sells his mill to buy an estate in the country, while all the time the weaver, who thinks he and his fellows are the real makers of this wealth, is struggling on for bread for their children, through their vicissitudes of lowered wages, short hours, fewer hands employed, *etc*.

'And when he knows trade is bad, and could understand (at least partially) that there are not buyers enough in the market to purchase the goods already made, and consequently that there is no demand for more; when he would bear and endure much without complaining, could he also see that his employers were bearing their share; he is, I say, bewildered and (to use his own words) "aggravated" to see that all goes on just as usual with the mill-owners. Large houses are still occupied, while spinners' and weavers' cottages stand empty, because the families that once occupied them are obliged to live in rooms or cellars.'

The Poor Law Amendment Act of 1834 meant that in future an able-bodied pauper would have to enter a workhouse if he wished to obtain relief. Widespread hostility was felt to the new law; many believed that life was harder in the workhouse than in prison. The Royal Commission on the Poor Laws had reported in 1834:

'The most pressing of the evils which we have described are those connected with the relief of the Able-bodied poor. They are the evils, therefore, for which we shall first propose remedies ... It may be assumed, that in the administration of relief, the public is warranted in imposing such conditions on the individuals relieved, as are conducive to the benefit of the individual himself, or of the country at large, at whose expense he is to be relieved.

'The first and most essential of all conditions ... is that his situation on the whole shall not be made really or apparently as eligible as the situation of the independent labourer of the lowest class ... nothing is necessary to arrest the progress of pauperism, except that all who receive relief from the parish should work for

An early effort at reform, model lodging-houses in Westminster, London, 1852

the parish exclusively, as hard and for less wages than independent labourers work for individual employers (20).'

Two years later, the Poor Law Commission reported that, in practice, the Act was meeting much opposition: 'It could not be expected, that an Act which so materially disturbed the distribution of as large a sum of money as £7,000,000 per annum, which of necessity changed the source from which a large portion of the inhabitants of the country derived their customary means of subsistence, and which in so doing opposed itself not only to the interests, the prejudices, and the fears of a large portion of the population, but pressed hardly on the sincere though mistaken notions of charity, which were established in the breasts of others, could possibly be carried into effect without difficulty and resistance. Your Lordship, therefore, will learn without surprise that the powers of the Act, and our means of carrying it into operation, have been put to the proof by every means which ingenuity could devise (21).'

Punch (1849) published a satirical song by Percival Leigh about the horrors of the workhouse. It was called 'The Pauper's Song':

A houseless, famish'd, desp'rate man,
A ragged wretch am I!
And how, and when, and where I can,
I feed, and lodge and lie.
And I must to the Workhouse go,
If better may not be;
Ay, if, indeed! The Workhouse? No!—
The Gaol—the Gaol for me!

The
workhouse
Charles Dickens agreed; the lot of the poor was very hard. One of his characters—Betty Higden—would sooner die than be caught and thrown in the workhouse: 'The day was cold and wet, but she [Betty Higden] scarcely knew it. She crept on, poor soul, like a criminal afraid of being taken, and felt little beyond the terror of falling down while it was yet daylight, and being found alive.

'She had no fear that she would live through another night. Sewn in the breast of her gown, the money to pay for her burial was still intact. If she could wear through the day, and then lie down to die under the cover of the darkness, she would die independent. If she were captured previously, the money would be taken from her as a pauper who had no right to it, and she would be carried to the accursed workhouse (22).'

Henry
Mayhew
It is surprising that the name Henry Mayhew is not more widely known, for, with the possible exception of Dickens, no writer more graphically described life amongst the poorer sections of London's population.

Mayhew was born in 1812—the same year as Dickens. He was to become a journalist. For a time he acted as joint-editor of *Punch*, but it is for his numerous articles that he is now remembered. Many of these were collected together and published, in 1851, under the title *London Labour and the London Poor*.

Coster-
mongers
One group of people about whom Mayhew wrote was the costermongers: 'The number of costermongers—that it is to say, of those street-sellers attending the London "green" and "fish" markets—appears to be, from the best data at my command, now 30,000 men, women and children. The costermongering class extends itself yearly; and it is computed that for the last five years it has increased considerably faster than the general metropolitan population. This increase is derived partly from *all* the children of

Inside the Field Lane Refuge, a workhouse, in 1859

costermongers following the father's trade, but chiefly from working men, such as the servants of greengrocers or of innkeepers, when out of employ, "taking a coster's barrow" for a livelihood; and the same being done by mechanics and labourers out of work. At the time of the famine in Ireland, it is calculated, that the number of Irish obtaining a living in the London streets must have been at least doubled …

'The street-sellers are to be seen in the greatest numbers at the London street markets on a Saturday night. Here, and in the shops immediately adjoining, the working-classes generally purchase their Sunday's dinner; and after pay-time on Saturday night, or early on Sunday morning, the crowd in the New-cut, and the Brill in particular, is almost impassable.

'Indeed, the scene in these parts has more of the character of a fair than a market. There are hundreds of stalls, and every stall has its one or two lights; either it is illuminated by the intense white light of the new self-generating gaslamp, or else it is brightened up by the red smoky flame of the old-fashioned grease lamp.

25

The market at Covent Garden, about 1820

Cockney slang   'The slang language of the costermongers is not very remarkable for originality of construction; it possesses no humour: but they boast that it is known only to themselves ...

A doogheno or dabheno	Is it a good or a bad market?
A regular trosseno	A regular bad one
On	No
Say	Yes
Tumble to your barrikin	Understand you
Top o'reeb	Pot of beer
Doing dab	Doing badly
Cool him	Look at him

'The latter phrase is used when one costermonger warns another of the approach of a policeman "who might order him to move on, or be otherwise unpleasant". "Cool" (look) is exclaimed, or "Cool him" (look at him). One costermonger told me as a great joke that a very stout policeman, who was then new to the duty, was when in a violent state of perspiration, much offended by a coster-monger saying "Cool him" (23).'

Mayhew wrote of his meetings with a strange variety of people: *Mr Tiffin and* crossing-sweepers ('we can scarcely walk along a street of any *Mr Black* extent, or pass through a square of the least pretensions to "gentility", without meeting one or more of these private scavengers'); cab-drivers; street-entertainers; 'mud-larks'; coal-heavers; chimney-sweeps; and many more. But surely the strangest of those with whom he spoke were Mr Tiffin and Mr Black:

'Perhaps the most eminent of the bug-destroyers in London is *Bug-* that of Messrs Tiffin and Son ... "Bug-Destroyers to Her Majesty *destroyer* and the Royal Family":

[Mr Tiffin said] 'I work for the upper classes only; that is, for carriage company and such-like approaches it, you know. I have noblemen's names, the first in England, on my books ... I've known persons to be laid up for a month through bug-bites. There was a very handsome fair young lady I knew once, and she was much bitten about the arms, and neck, and face, so that her eyes were so swelled up she couldn't see. The spots rose up like blisters, the same as if stung with a nettle, only on a very large scale. The bites were much inflamed, and after a time they had the appearance of boils ...

'I was once at work on the Princess Charlotte's bedstead. I was in the room, and she asked me if I had found anything, and I told her no; but just at that minute I *did* happen to catch one, and upon that she sprang up on the bed, and put her hand on my shoulder, to look at it. She had been tormented by the creature, because I was ordered to come directly, and that was the only one I found.

'When the Princess saw it, she said, "Oh, the nasty thing! That's what tormented me last night; don't let him escape." I think he looked all the better for having tasted royal blood.'

'I sought an interview with Mr "Jack" Black, whose hand-bills *Mole-* are headed—"V.R. Rat and mole destroyer to Her Majesty." ... *destroyer* I was soon at home with Mr Black. He was a very different man from what I had expected to meet, for there was an expression of kindliness in his countenance, a quality which does not exactly agree with one's preconceived notions of ratcatchers.'

Mr Black told Mayhew, "I should think I've been ratting a'most for five-and-thirty year; indeed, I may say from my childhood, for I've kept at it a'most all my life. I've been dead near three times from bites—as near as a toucher. I once had the teeth of a rat break in my finger, which was dreadful bad, and swole, and putrified, so that I had to have the broken bits pulled out with tweezers ...

"The first rats I caught was when I was about nine years of age ... I wasn't afraid to handle rats even then; it seemed to come nat'ral to me. I very soon had some in my pocket, and some in my hands, carrying them away as fast as I could, and putting them into my wire cage ... After that I bought some ferrets ...

"I also exterminate moles for Her Majesty." (24)'

Chartism: 'discontent grown fierce'

Mayhew was a skilled writer, and drew his London characters with sympathy. But over England as a whole, poverty was making industrial workers restless. The golden promises of life in the towns had been broken. Packed together in jerry-built terraced houses, their discontent grew fierce and vocal in a way that it never could have done in the countryside. Riots and strikes broke out with alarming frequency in the thirties and forties. Machinery was smashed. Vast crowds gathered in the towns and cities to shout their protests.

Chartism, with its demand for a charter of rights from parliament, became the biggest rallying point. An eye-witness observer described its mass appeal:

'In the autumn of 1838 the meetings began to assume a formidable character ... there were no rooms to be obtained capable of holding the dense crowds who were every day more anxious to express their hatred of the existing system, and the Town Halls were almost always refused. There is a way out of every difficulty, and a project speedily suggested itself to the minds of the leading men which would make them independent of all halls and places for indoor meetings.

'They suggested the holding of meetings by torch-light, as being better suited to the people's convenience, both as regards time and expense. The expedient was but little sooner suggested than adopted, and for a short period the factory districts presented a series of such imposing popular demonstrations, as were perhaps never witnessed in any previous agitation.

'Bolton, Stockport, Ashton, Hyde, Stalybridge, Leigh, and various other places, large and small, were the scenes of these magnificent gatherings. At the whole of them, the working people met in their thousands and tens of thousands to swear devotion to the common cause. It is almost impossible to imagine the excitement ...'

To understand 'the public feeling, it was necessary to be an eye-witness of the proceedings. The people did not go singly to the place of meeting but met in a body at a starting point, from whence, at a given time, they issued in huge numbers, formed into procession, traversing the principal streets, making the heavens echo with the thunder of their cheers on recognising the idols of their worship in the men who were to address them, and sending forth volleys of the most hideous groans on passing the office of some hostile news-paper, or the house of some obnoxious magistrate or employer.

'The banners containing the more formidable devices, viewed by the red light of the glaring torches, presented a scene of awful grandeur. The death's heads represented on some of them grinned like ghostly spectres, and served to remind many a mammon-worshipper of his expected doom (25).'

'All London is making preparations to encounter a Chartist row tomorrow,' wrote Charles Greville in his Diary on 9 April 1848. 'All the clerks in the different offices are ordered to be sworn in special constables, and to constitute themselves into garrisons ... We are to pass the whole day at the office tomorrow, and I am to send down all my guns; in short, we are to take a warlike attitude ... Every gentleman in London is become a constable, and there is an organisation of some sort in every district.' *Greville on Chartism*

Thomas Carlyle wrote during those troubled times: 'Chartism means the bitter discontent grown fierce and mad ... It is a new name for a thing which has had many names (26).' *Carlyle*

What sort of people were the Chartists? In a novel, the famous author Charles Kingsley expressed the mixed feelings shared by many: 'I shrank from him at first, when I heard him called a Chartist; for my dim notions of that class were, that they were a very wicked set of people, who wanted to kill all the soldiers and policemen, and respectable people, and rob all the shops of their contents. But, Chartist or none, Crossthwaite fascinated me (27).'

The Chartists were fighting for radical political reforms. To many people they were out-and-out revolutionaries—demanding

29

Summoning colliers' wives to a meeting during a colliery strike

six points: a vote for all adult males in the country, ballots to be held secretly, annual elections of parliament, abolition of the property qualifications for MPs, payment of MPs and equal electoral districts. They marched with petitions to Parliament in 1838, 1842 and 1848. Here is an extract from the petition of 1838:

Political Reforms

'We, your petitioners, dwell in a land whose merchants are noted for their enterprise, whose manufacturers are very skilful and whose workmen are proverbial for their industry. The land itself is goodly, the soil rich, and the temperature wholesome. It is abundantly furnished with the materials of commerce and trade. It has numerous and convenient harbours. In facility of internal communication it excels all others. For three and twenty years we have enjoyed a profound peace.

'Yet with all the elements of national prosperity, and with every disposition to take advantage of them, we find ourselves overwhelmed with public and private suffering. We are bowed down under a load of taxes, which, notwithstanding, fall greatly short of the wants of our rulers. Our traders are trembling on the verge of bankruptcy; our workmen are starving. Capital brings no profit, and labour no remuneration. The home of the artificer is desolate, and the warehouse of the pawnbroker is full. The workhouse is full, and the manufactory is deserted.

'We have looked on every side; we have searched diligently in order to find out the causes of distress so sore and so long continued. We can discover none in nature or in Providence ...

'Required, as we are universally, to support and obey the laws, nature and reason entitle us to demand that in the making of the laws the universal voice shall be implicitly listened to. We perform the duties of freedom; we must have the privileges of free men (28).'

Parliament, however, became even more worried when it heard that the petition was a fraudulent one:

Forged Petitions

'The Hon. Member for Nottingham (Mr F. O'Connor) stated on presenting the petition, that 5,706,000 names were attached to it; but upon the most careful examination ... the number of signatures has been ascertained to be 1,975,496. It is further evident to your Committee that on numerous consecutive sheets the signatures are in one and the same handwriting. Your Committee also observed the names of distinguished individuals attached to the petition, who can scarcely be supposed to concur to its prayer: among which occurs the name of Her Majesty, as Victoria Rex, April 1st, F.M. Duke of Wellington, Sir Robert Peel, *etc.*

'Your Committee have also observed, in derogation of the value of such petition, the insertion of numbers of names which are obviously fictitious, such as "No Cheese", "Pug Nose", "Flat Nose". There are others included, which your Committee do not hazard offending the House and the dignity and the decency of their own proceedings by reporting (29).'

Many people believed that food would be cheaper if Britain adopted a policy of free trade. They especially disliked the Corn Laws, which kept out foreign wheat until the price of home-grown wheat had risen very high. This seemed to protect rich farmers at the expense of everyone else. Industrialists, in fact, were anxious to have these laws repealed, for expensive bread forced up wages.

Against the Corn Laws

In 1838, Richard Cobden and John Bright, two factory owners, were amongst those who formed the Anti-Corn Law League. Here are popular verses in favour of free trade (30):

> Why are ye called 'My Lord', and 'Squire'
> While fed by mine and me,
> And wringing food, and clothes, and fire
> From bread taxed misery?

> Dear Sugar, dear Tea, and dear Corn,
> Conspired with dear Representation
> To laugh worth and honour to scorn,
> And beggar the whole British Nation.

Richard
Cobden

'The single and undisputed object of the League', said Richard Cobden, 'is to put down commercial monopoly; but that cannot be done by saddling upon our backs a fixed duty on corn which means a differential duty on sugar, on coffee, and monopoly in every other article. The Corn-law is the great tree of Monopoly, under whose baneful shadow every other restriction exists. Cut it down by the roots and it will destroy the others in its fall. The sole object of the League is to put an end to and extinguish once and forever, the principle of maintaining taxes for the benefit of a particular class ...'

'Free Trade!' shouted Richard Cobden enthusiastically. 'What is it? Why, breaking down the barriers that separate nations; Those barriers behind which nestle the feelings of pride, revenge, hatred and jealousy, which every now and then burst their bounds, and deluge whole countries with blood; those feelings which nourish the poison of war and conquest, which assert that without conquest we can have no trade ...

'It was because of the moral bearing of this question, that I take pride and gratification in forming one in the present agitation; and I invite you all to take a part in it, for there is room and glory and fame enough for all as soon as we have achieved the great triumph! (31)'

Irish potato
famine

In 1846, faced with an appalling potato famine in Ireland, Sir Robert Peel, the prime minister, saw no choice but to repeal the Corn Laws. This angered some of his party, including Disraeli, who claimed that he had betrayed them: 'What happens in this country?' asked Disraeli. 'A body of gentlemen, able and adroit men, come forward, and profess contrary doctrines to those of these new economists [the League]. They place themselves at the head of that great popular party who are adverse to the new ideas, and, professing their opinions, they climb and clamber into power by having accepted, or rather by having eagerly sought the trust.

'It follows that the body whom they represent ... conclude that their opinions are represented in the State ... we trusted to others.' He added bitterly, 'I think the right Hon. Baronet [Peel] may congratulate himself on his complete success in having entirely deceived his party (32).'

What was life really like for those who lived in the new industrial *In the new* towns of the North and Midlands? The scene was a grim one. *towns* Overcrowded houses were packed together in narrow streets and courts which were often piled deep in rotting refuse. Frederick Engels reported that in Manchester:

'The cottages are old, dirty, and of the smallest sort, the streets uneven, fallen into ruts, and in parts without drains or pavement; masses of refuse, offal, and sickening filth lie among standing pools in all directions; the atmosphere is poisoned by the effluvia from these, laden and darkened by the smoke of a dozen tall factory chimneys. A horde of ragged women and children swarm about here, as filthy as the swine that thrive upon the garbage heaps and in the puddles ...

'The race that lives in these ruinous cottages, behind broken windows mended with oilskins, spring doors, and rotten doorposts, or in dark, wet cellars, in measureless filth and stench, in this atmosphere penned in as if with a purpose, this race must really have reached the lowest stage of humanity. This is the impression and the line of thought which the exterior of this district forces upon the beholder.

'But what must one think when he hears that in each of these pens, containing at most two rooms, a garret, and perhaps a cellar, on the average twenty human beings live; that in the whole region, for each one hundred and twenty persons, one usually inaccessible privy is provided (33).'

The famous public health reformer Edwin Chadwick found *Chadwick* similar conditions in Stockton: 'Shepherd's Buildings consist of two rows of houses with a street seven yards wide between them;

each row consists of what are styled back and front houses—that is two houses placed back to back. There are no yards or out-conveniences; the privies are in the centre of each row, about a yard wide.'

His report went on to say that 'each house consists of two rooms, viz., a house place and a sleeping-room above; each room is about three yards wide and four long ... There are forty-four houses in the two rows, and twenty-two cellars, all of the same size. The cellars are let off as separate dwellings; these are dark, damp, and very low, not more than six feet between the ceiling and the floor.

'The street between the two rows is seven yards wide, in the centre of which is the common gutter, or more properly sink, into which all sorts of refuse is thrown; it is a foot in depth. Thus there is always a quantity of putrefying matter contaminating the air ... In many of these dwellings there are four persons in one bed (34).'

Charles Dickens painting a fictional scene had no need to exaggerate the truth: '[Coketown] was a town of red brick, or of brick that would have been red if the smoke and ashes allowed it; but as matters stood it was a town of unnatural red and black, like the painted face of a savage. It was a town of machinery and tall chimneys ... it had a black canal in it, and a river that ran purple with ill-smelling dye (35).'

In such conditions, one need not wonder at the serious cholera *Public health* epidemic of 1832. At last, people began to take the question of public health seriously. The newly-formed Poor Law Commission drew attention to the links between poverty, disease and insanitary conditions: 'In general, all epidemics and all infectious disease are attended with charges immediate and ultimate, on the poor rates. Labourers are suddenly thrown, by infectious disease, into a state of destitution, for which immediate relief must be given. In the case of death, the widow and children are thrown as paupers on the parish (36).'

Edwin Chadwick, the Commission's Secretary, made his own famous report four years later, in 1842, noting: 'broken panes in every window-frame, and filth and vermin in every nook. With the walls unwhitewashed for years, black with the smoke of foul chimneys, without water, with corded bed-stocks for beds, and

35

Facing page Labourers dwellings in Birmingham in the 1870's

Squalid tenements near the River Thames, London

sacking for bed-clothing, with floors unwashed from year to year ...

Outside, 'there are streets, elevated a foot, sometimes two, above the level of the causeway, by the accumulation of years, and stagnant puddles here and there, with their foetid exhalations, causeways broken and dangerous, ash-places choked up with filth, and excrementitious deposits on all sides as a consequence, undrained, unpaved, unventilated, uncared-for by any authority but the landlord, who weekly collects his miserable rents from his miserable tenants.

'Can we wonder that such places are the hot-beds of disease,' he asked, and so cause 'the mortality which Leeds exhibits? (37)'

The young and disease

The young, he noted, were especially prone to disease: 'It is an appalling fact that, of all who are born of the labouring classes in Manchester, more than 57 per cent die before they attain five years of age; that is, before they can be engaged in factory labour, or in

36

any other labour ... Of 4,629 deaths of persons of the labouring classes who died in the year 1840 in Manchester, the numbers were at the several periods as follows:

Under 5 years of age	2,649
Above 5 years and under 10	215
Above 10 years and under 15	107
Above 15 years and under 20	135'

Chadwick found (37) that life was healthier in rural areas: 'To compare the chances of life between a crowded manufacturing population and a less crowded rural population, I selected the county of Rutland [and] ... Manchester:

	AVERAGE AGE OF DEATH	
	In Manchester	In Rutlandshire
	Years	*Years*
Professional persons and gentry, and their families	38	52
Tradesmen and their families. (In Rutlandshire, farmers and graziers are included with shopkeepers)	20	41
Mechanics, labourers, and their families	17	38'

So it was that the 1840s were years of crisis. The character of *Years of crisis* English life was being transformed by industrial expansion, and by great movements of population towards urban life. New problems of food and of public health were faced by a parliamentary and economic system better suited to the eighteenth century. The mass violence of this decade was its symptom.

What was to be the cure? The answers still lay many years in the future. Before that time Victorian England was to face one of its greatest crises—that of employment, and conditions of life in mines, mills and factories. It is to these conditions that we will now turn.

3 'Hard Times'

THE NEW towns, products of the Industrial Revolution grew at a rapid pace. The population of Bradford rose from 44,000 in 1831 to 104,000 in 1851; Sheffield from 92,000 to 135,000; Blackburn from 27,000 to 65,000; and Manchester and Salford from 237,000 to 400,000. In the towns the newcomers had to adjust to a different way of life. This was nowhere more marked than in the factories where many now worked. *Working population*

One writer gives a graphic account of factory life in a book published in early industrial times: 'Any man who has stood at twelve o'clock at the single narrow doorway, which serves as the place of exit for the hands employed in the great cotton-mills, must acknowledge that an uglier set of men and women, of boys and girls, taken them in the mass, it would be impossible to congregate in a smaller compass. Their complexion is sallow and pallid.

'Their stature low—the average height of four hundred men, measured at different times, and at different places, being five feet six inches. Their limbs slender, and playing badly and ungracefully. A very general bowing of the legs. Great numbers of girls and women walking lamely or awkwardly, with raised chests and spinal flexures. Nearly all have flat feet, accompanied with a down-tread, differing very widely from the elasticity of action in the foot and ankle, attendant upon perfect formation ...'

He continues thus: 'The mode of life which the system of labour ... forces upon the operative, is one singularly unfavourable to domesticity. Rising at or before day-break, between four and five o'clock the year round, scarcely refreshed by his night's repose, he swallows a hasty meal, or hurries to the mill without taking

39

Facing page Payday. Wages remained low because unemployment was high

any food whatever. At eight o'clock half an hour, and in some instances forty minutes, are allowed for breakfast. In many cases, the engine continues at work during mealtime, obliging the labourer to eat and still overlook his work ... After this he is incessantly engaged—not a single minute of rest or relaxation being allowed him.

Working hours 'At twelve o'clock the engine stops, and an hour is given for dinner. The hands leave the mill, and seek their homes, where this meal is usually taken ... If, as it often happens, the majority of the labourers reside at some distance, a great portion of the allotted time is necessarily taken up by the walk, or rather run, backwards and forwards ...

'Again they are closely immured from one o'clock till eight or nine, with the exception of twenty minutes, this being allowed for tea, or baggin-time, as it is called. This imperfect meal is almost universally taken in the mill: it consists of tea and wheaten bread, with very few exceptions. During the whole of this long period they are actively and unremittingly engaged in a crowded room and an elevated temperature, so that, when finally dismissed for the day, they are exhausted equally in body and mind.

'It must be remembered that father, mother, son, and daughter, are alike engaged; no one capable of working is spared to make home (to which, after a day of such toil and privation, they are hastening) comfortable and desirable (38).'

Factory conditions Factory work was dangerous, too. Factory legislation was virtually non-existent, and companies had almost no obligations towards their employees. Unhealthy conditions in many mills produced many new chest and lung diseases for which there was no cure. In addition, operatives faced the constant risk of accidents from inadequately fenced machines: 'In many of the cotton and flax-spinning mills, the air is filled with fibrous dust, which produces chest infection, especially among workers in the carding and combing rooms ... The most common effects of this breathing of dust are blood-spitting, hard, noisy breathing, pains in the chest, coughs, sleeplessness—in short, all the symptoms of asthma, ending in the worst cases in consumption ...

'The most common accident is the squeezing off of a single joint of a finger, somewhat less common the loss of the whole finger,

The Atlantic submarine cable being made at a Greenwich factory in 1857

half or a whole hand, an arm, *etc.*, in the machinery. Lockjaw very often follows …

'Besides the deformed persons, a great number of maimed ones may be seen going about in Manchester; this one has lost an arm or part of one, that one a foot, the third half a leg; it is like living in the midst of an army just returned from a campaign (39).'

Workers were often cheated by unscrupulous employers. One angry worker, James Leach, produced a book on the subject, in which he gave some examples: *Unscrupulous employers*

'It often happens that when the weaver goes to work in the morning, he finds the clock fifteen minutes forwarder than when he left in the evening. The hands on the factory clock do not always move from "internal wheels", but very frequently from a little external aid; this always takes place after the hands have left the mill in the evening …

41

'The reader will best understand why this is done, when we inform him that thirty or forty people may be frequently seen at the lodge door locked out, in the morning, while the person with the "fine-book" has been through the rooms of the mill, taking down the numbers of the looms of those that were absent.

'[We once] counted ninety-five persons that were thus locked out at half-past five o'clock in the morning. The way in which this method of "genteel robbery" was accomplished was by putting the clock half an hour forward—that is, it was fifteen minutes later than the public clocks of the town in the evening, and fifteen minutes forwarder in the morning. These ninety-five persons were fined three-pence each (40).'

Enlightened employers

But if many factory owners showed little concern for the well-being of their workers, others were more enlightened. Also from Manchester, Leon Faucher wrote: 'Mr T. Ashton employs 1,500 work-people, of both sexes. One immense room, filled with looms, contains four hundred of them. The young women are well and decently clothed. A sort of large apron, extending from the shoulders to the feet, protects their outer garments from dirt ... The houses inhabited by the work-people form long and large streets. Mr Ashton has built three hundred of them, which he lets at 3s or 3s 6d per week ... The proprietor furnishes, at his own charge, water to the houses, keeps them in good repair, and pays the local rates (41).'

Children in factories

Thousands of children worked in the factories of Scotland and the North. Very few ever went to school. Although boys and girls were not supposed to start work until they were at least six years old, many began at a younger age. Their hours were long and their tasks monotonous. To this hard routine might be added the cruelty of the overseer.

The Report of Commissioners on the employment of children in factories (1833) gives evidence: 'The Commissioners have everywhere investigated with the utmost care the treatment to which children are subjected while engaged in the labour of the factory. These inquiries have obtained from the children themselves, from their parents, from operatives, overlookers, proprietors, medical practitioners, and magistrates, such statements amongst others as the following:

42

'"When she was a child too little to put on her ain claithes the overlooker used to beat her till she screamed again."

'"Gets many a good beating and swearing. They are all very ill used. The overseer carries a strap."

'"Has been licked four or five times."

'"The boys are often severely strapped; the girls sometimes get a clout. The mothers often complain of this. Has seen the boys have black and blue marks after strapping."

'"Three weeks ago the overseer struck him in the eye with his clenched fist so as to force him to be absent two days; another overseer used to beat him with his fist, striking him so that his arm was black and blue."

'"Has often seen the workers beat cruelly. Has seen the girls strapped; but the boys were beat so that they fell to the floor in the course of the beating, with a rope with four tails, called a cat. Has seen the boys black and blue, crying for mercy."'

Struck with a guilty conscience, Joseph Badder, a spinner, also gave evidence to the Commissioners: 'I have frequently had complaints against myself by the parents of children for beating them. I used to beat them. I am sure that no man can do without it who works long hours; I am sure he cannot. I told them I was very sorry after I had done it, but I was forced to it. The master expected me to do my work, and I could not do mine unless they did theirs ...

'I have seen them fall asleep, and they have been performing their work with their hands while they were asleep, after the billy had stopped, when their work was over. I have stopped and looked at them for two minutes, going through the motions of piecening fast asleep, when there was really no work to do, and they were really doing nothing (42).'

Further evils are recounted by a factory inspector: 'No arrangements of the best-intentioned master could prevent the evils inherent in a system which deprived children of that fair proportion of air and exercise natural to their time of life, and without which their chance of growing up in health and strength must at least have been considerably diminished, and which cut them off from all opportunity of being properly educated (43).'

Factories were not the only places where children were exploited. Many worked in coal mines. The first official report stated: 'We

find, in regard to COAL MINES:

'That instances occur in which Children are taken into these mines to work as early as four years of age, sometimes at five, and between five and six, not unfrequently between six and seven, and often from seven to eight, while from eight to nine is the ordinary age at which employment in these mines commences ...

'That in several districts female children begin to work in these mines at the same early ages as the males (44).'

J. R. Leifchild wrote in *Our Coal Fields and Our Pits* (1853) how boys became valuable property: 'Families of *boys* are, amongst pit-people, valuable property, on account of their earnings in the pits. A widow with a family of boys is considered a "catch". I was told that such a widow was accosted by a suitor even at her husband's grave. Her reply was, "You are too late: I am engaged. I accepted B. before starting for the funeral!"'

Other children were employed in nail-making: 'Boy, aged 12: works at nails; has worked at it above a year and a half, and gets from 3s 6d to 4s a week. His mother takes the nails he makes into the warehouse, and gets the money ... Some of the boys are not well treated by their masters; they don't get enough victuals, and some are beat. *More child exploitation*

'Knows a boy that makes scraps [bad nails], and somebody in the warehouse took him and put his head down on an iron counter and hammered a nail through one ear, and the boy made good nails ever since (45).'

And in the Staffordshire potteries not only were the hours tremendously long, but the temperatures rose to almost unbearable heights: 'The class of children whose physical condition has the strongest claims to consideration is that of the "jiggers" and "mould runners", who, by the very nature of their work, are rendered pale, weak, diminutive, and unhealthy; they are employed by the dish, saucer, and plate makers; their hours are from half-past five in the morning to six at night, but in numberless instances they are required to labour on to eight, nine, or ten, and this in an atmosphere varying from 100 to 120 degrees. (46)' *Staffordshire*

Some boys and girls, chosen for their size and agility, became chimney-sweeps. Perhaps one of the best-known in Victorian fiction was Tom, in Charles Kingsley's *Water Babies* (1863). To *'The Water Babies'*

45

Facing page Working conditions for women and children in the coal mines, 1840s, illustrations from the *Coal Commission Report*

modern readers, this appears an extremely sentimental book, but perhaps sentiment was the only answer to the brutalities:

'[Tom] cried half his life, and laughed the other half. He cried when he had to climb the dark flues, rubbing his poor knees and elbows raw; and when the soot got into his eyes, which it did every day in the week; and when his master beat him, which he did every day in the week; and when he had not enough to eat, which happened every day in the week likewise. And he laughed the other half of the day, when he was tossing halfpennies with the other boys, or playing leapfrog over the posts, or bowling stones at the horses' legs as they trotted by.'

One has to remember that, in the early 1800s, most MPs believed that Parliament had no right to interfere in industrial matters. Not until 1833 was an effective 'Act to Regulate the Labour of Children and Young Persons in the Mills and Factories' passed. Inspectors were appointed to see that its provisions were carried out. *Parliament acts*

Further Acts followed in 1844 and 1847; the first reduced the working hours of children who were under thirteen, while the second lowered the working day of women and young persons.

Here are the key extracts from the Act of 1833: 'Whereas it is necessary that the Hours of Labour of Children and young Persons employed in Mills and Factories should be regulated, inasmuch as there are great Numbers of Children and young Persons now employed in Mills and Factories, and their Hours of Labour are longer than is desirable, due Regard being had to their Health and Means of Education; be it therefore enacted ...

'That ... no Person under Eighteen Years of Age shall be allowed to work in the Night ... in or about any Cotton, Woollen, Worsted, Hemp, Flax, Tow, Linen, or Silk Mill or Factory wherein Steam or Water or any mechanical Power is or shall be used to propel or work the Machinery ... That ... no Person under the Age of Eighteen Years shall be employed in any such Mill or Factory ... more than Twelve Hours in any One Day, nor more than Sixty-Nine hours in any One Week ...

'That ... it shall not be lawful for any Person whatsoever to employ in any Factory or Mill as aforesaid, except in Mills for the Manufacture of Silk, any Child who shall not have completed his

47

Facing page Boy chimney sweeps seeking work in the 1860s

or her Ninth Year of Age ...

'That ... it shall not be lawful for any Person whatsoever to employ, keep, or allow to remain in any Factory or Mill, as aforesaid, for a longer Time than Forty-eight Hours in any One Week, nor for a longer Time than Nine Hours in any One Day ... any Child who shall not have completed his or her Thirteenth Year of Age ...

'That ... every child herein-before restricted to the Performance of Forty-eight Hours of Labour in any One Week shall ... attend some School.'

A boy factory hand making lace tags, 1844

Ashley's speech (*1846*)   On 29 January 1846, Lord Ashley spoke up in the House of Commons on behalf of 'young persons': 'Among all the alterations that have been effected since the year 1833, I am sorry to perceive that nothing has been done for the benefit of young persons between the ages of thirteen and eighteen. Those young persons are exposed under the existing law to twelve hours' actual labour per day; now a very large portion of them are females …

'I appeal to the House to say, whether it is not cruel to take a young female on the very day on which she has passed the age of thirteen, at the most tender period of her life, and to demand of her precisely the same work in duration, and frequently the same

Children operating an envelope machine

in intensity, which is demanded from ripe and vigorous manhood?' (47).

Lord Ashley, who became the seventh Earl of Shaftesbury in 1851, was a wealthy landowner. His own parents treated him cruelly, and the school to which he was sent was little better than Dotheboys Hall in Dicken's *Nicholas Nickleby* (see p. 62). Perhaps it was his childhood experiences which made him fight so hard to reduce the misery of others.

Ashley not only played a leading part in improving factory conditions. In June 1842, he introduced a Bill which would prohibit women, girls, and boys under ten, from ever working below ground:

'Sir, it is not possible for any man, whatever be his station, if he have but a heart within his bosom, to read the details of this awful document [the Report of the Royal Commission on Women and Children in Mines] without a combined feeling of shame, terror, and indignation ... The first provision ... I shall propose will be the total exclusion of all females from the mines and collieries ...

'I think that every principle of religion—I think that every law of nature calls for such a step; and I know of no argument that can be raised against it, unless one of a most unworthy and of a completely selfish character (48).'

Incidentally, he felt deeply, too, about the mentally sick, and promoted legislation to provide care for these 'desolate and oppressed creatures'. The lunatic asylums of the day were little more than prisons. At the most notorious, Bethlehem Hospital in London (popularly nicknamed Bedlam), tourists could pay a twopenny admission fee and spend a few hours teasing the inmates.

In July 1844 Ashley pleaded in Parliament for a more humane attitude:

'We must not run away with the notion that even the hopelessly mad are dead to all capacity of intellectual or moral exertion—quite the reverse; their feelings, too, are painfully alive ... Their condition appeals to our highest sympathies, "Majestic, though in ruin"; for though there may be, in the order of a merciful Providence, some compensating dispensation which abates within, the horrors manifested without, we must judge alone by what we see.

'I trust, therefore that I shall stand excused, though I have consumed so much of your valuable time, when you call to mind that the motion is made on behalf of the most helpless, if not the most afflicted, portion of the human race (49).'

Ragged School Movement

Ashley (Shaftesbury) was a prominent supporter of the Ragged School Movement. These schools catered for 'wild, rough, uncouth' children whom no other school would accept. To Ashley, schools of any kind not only meant a little education, but release from a barbaric life in mines and factories. Dickens admired much that this reformer did, but had reservations about some of his schemes. He doubted, for example, whether ragged schools could ever provide a satisfactory system of education for the poor:

'I have no desire to praise the system pursued in the Ragged Schools; which is necessarily very imperfect, if indeed there be one. So far as I have any means of judging of what is taught there, I should individually object to it, as not being sufficiently secular, and as presenting too many religious mysteries and difficulties, to minds not sufficiently prepared for their reception.

'But I should very imperfectly discharge in myself the duty I wish to urge and impress on others, if I allowed any such doubt of mine to interfere with my appreciation of the efforts of these teachers, or my true wish to promote them by any slight means in my power (50).' In a letter to Miss Burdett-Coutts, he wrote of Ashley as 'a kind of amiable bull in a china shop of good intentions (51).'

But one thing was clear. If any radical improvement was to be made in the quality of life in the large urban centres like Manchester, Liverpool, Sheffield, Birmingham, Bolton and elsewhere, something would have to be done about the education of the poorer classes. A few farsighted people saw, too, that it was a practical as well as a moral issue.

A practical issue

Above A charitable Quaker School, and *below* a Ragged School

4 Unwillingly to School

FOR THE children of the poor—often called the 'lower orders'—
there were various private venture schools, like 'dame schools'
and 'common day schools'. Not surprisingly, the low fees went
hand in hand with teaching of a very poor standard.

A school inspector, the Rev. Allen, recalls one of these private
schools: '[I was] directed to a room in the rear of a shop, about
ten feet by twelve, in which, with my hat on, I could barely stand
upright; the floor was crowded with benches, on which some dozen
children were sitting in ranks closely packed, many without any
means of employing their time. The mistress was in the shop,
having left the children in the care of a girl who was standing
amidst the crowd with an infant in her arms; the atmosphere was
so oppressive and disagreeable that I could not wonder at the
teacher finding excuses for being absent from her post (52).'

James Kay-Shuttleworth believed most schoolmasters would
consider they were lacking in their duty if they showed any kindness
to the children: 'As far as I have observed, generally, of the common
day schools in large towns, in the north and elsewhere, it appears to
me that the whole system is defective in this respect, that it is supposed that education will be best promoted by coercion ... that
knowledge is in itself repulsive, and that it requires coercive treatment to make a child acquire even the simplest elements of knowledge; and as far as respects kindness in the treatment of children,
I think the great majority of such schoolmasters would conceive
that they deserted their duty if they treated the children kindly
(53).'

Of greater interest, however, were the schools of two religious

53

societies, the National Society, founded by Anglicans, and the British and Foreign Society, run by Nonconformists: these had been founded early in the century. After 1833 both received small government grants and in 1839 inspectors—HMI's—were appointed to visit and report on schools. One of the things the inspectors found, was an almost total lack of books and classroom equipment:

'The want of fit and proper books on secular subjects may be considered amongst the chief obstacles to the progress of education

The popular image of fierce schoolmasters, early nineteenth century

in our National Schools ... The entire want of useful apparatus has been a great hindrance to the advance of science ... Even from the want of a simple blackboard, the study of arithmetic, linear drawing, and vocal music has been impeded; whilst an almost incredible extent of ignorance in geography, both local and general, has been occasioned by the absence of maps and globes (54).'

Another school inspector, J. Fletcher, reported mass absenteeism: 'The school committees cannot, and the parents will not, enforce regular attendance; they say that their elder children being in the mill, they cannot send their younger children regularly.

Even many who do come attend only on condition that they leave at certain hours to take the meals of their parents, brothers or sisters to the factories (55).'

Yet, despite this absenteeism, classes were impossibly over-crowded. Classes of over a hundred were very common. Another of the inspectors had a tentative proposal to make about this: 'I wish to see no school room, except, perhaps, such as are built for infants, constructed for more than 100 children, and I believe that a smaller number, as eighty, will afford sufficient work for a good master (56).'

Crowded classes

Physical violence was commonly indulged in by school masters and mistresses: 'I have witnessed a master step into a class where was some little inattention or disturbance, and deal out boxes on the ear, blows on the head, and cuffs on the back, promiscuously on all within his reach, and then, as though he had done all that duty required him, return to his seat. Sometimes abuse is uttered in the same way, as, e.g., "You, John ———, are the worst boy in school; everybody knows it, and I am sure you will come to no good", *etc.* In more than one instance I have pained with hearing the faults of parents cast forth publicly before the school, as matters of reflection upon their children (57).'

School teachers

The Rev. Allen reports, in the Minutes of the Committee of Council on Education (1841–2), of the difficulty of recruiting teachers: 'If the village schoolmaster be worse paid than the village carpenter or blacksmith, what hope is there of finding any but the most incompetent person in the former situation?' And adds: 'The great want is that of properly trained teachers.'

In 1846, mainly due to the efforts of James Kay-Shuttleworth, the first teachers' training scheme was introduced. Pupil-teachers were apprenticed to experienced headmasters and headmistresses for five years. When this time was up, the apprentice could gain entry to a normal school (training college) by passing the Queen's Scholarship Examination:

Apprentice teachers

'Their Lordships had further under their consideration the Report of the Inspectors of Schools, memorials from certain Boards of Education, and letters from the clergy and others, representing the very early age at which the children acting as assistants to schoolmasters are withdrawn from school to manual labour.' They felt that benefits 'would arise if such scholars as might be distinguished by proficiency and good conduct were apprenticed to skilful masters, to be instructed and trained, so as to be prepared to complete their education as schoolmasters in a Normal School (58).'

Teaching improved in the National and British schools. But in the common venture schools, standards stayed at rock bottom. As for the teachers: 'None are too old, too poor, too ignorant, too feeble, too sickly, too unqualified in one or every way, to regard themselves, and to be regarded by others, as unfit for school-keeping. Nay, there are few, if any, occupations regarded as incompatible with school-keeping, if not simultaneous, at least as preparatory employments (59).'

'All the Year Round'

The trouble was, the status of the teacher was negligible (60):

> If you would know the Schoolmaster,
> He wears a suit of black,
> The cuffs and button-holes are worn,
> And it shines adown his back.
>
> Bent is he now, and tall, and thin;
> His bushy brows are grey:
> The light that once had place within
> His eyes has shrunk away ...
>
> He hath no money, hath no wife
> To cheer his lonely hours;
> No patron ever saw in him
> The scholar's noblest powers.
>
> Grim Patience is his heritage,
> And Poverty his lot;
> And so he is outstripped by all,
> And is by all forgot!

Grammar schools

For the professional and business classes there were about five hundred grammar schools to which they could send their sons. They were mostly day schools, and the parents had to pay fees. These schools, which had few places for girls, were often attacked for the subjects they taught: 'If we find in the country and town schools little preparation for occupations, still less for the future agriculturalist or mechanic, we find in the Grammar Schools much

56

Facing page A schoolroom near Regent's Park, London, in 1870 *above* and the New Free Grammar and Commercial School at Loughborough, 1850 *below*

greater defects. The middle class in all its sections, except the more learned professions, finds no instruction which can suit its middle class wants. They are fed with the dry husks of ancient learning when they should be taking sound and substantial food from the great treasury of modern discovery.

'The applications of mechanical and chemical science to everyday wants—such a study as will show the progress of civilisation— and such knowledge of public economy in the large sense of the term as will guard them against the delusions of political fanatics and knaves, and lead to a due understanding of their position in society, are all subjects worth as much labour and enquiry to that great body, as a little Latin learnt in a very imperfect manner, with some scraps of Greek to boot—the usual stunted course of most of our Grammar Schools (61).'

For the upper classes and the very rich, there were the great public *Public schools* schools, most of which, like Eton, Winchester and Harrow, were ancient foundations richly endowed. The nineteenth century was the hey-day of the public schools, whose virtues—of character-building and organisation—were regarded as the virtues of the age, and which provided a ruling élite not only in Britain, but in the vast Victorian empire overseas.

Some public schools were made great by their autocratic head-masters, the most celebrated of whom was Dr Arnold of Rugby School. Rugby School provided the setting for Thomas Hughes' bestseller, *Tom Brown's Schooldays* (1857) possibly the best mirror of public school life at that time. Here is Tom's arrival for the first time at the school gates:

'"And so here's Rugby, sir, at last, and you'll be in plenty of time for dinner at the School-house, as I told you," said the old guard ...

'Tom's heart beat quick as he passed the great school-field or close, with its noble elms, in which several games at football were going on, and tried to take in at once the long line of gray buildings, beginning with the chapel, and ending with the School-house, the residence of the headmaster, where the great flag was lazily waving from the highest round tower. And he began already to be proud of being a Rugby boy, as he passed the school-gates, with the oriel window above, and saw the boys standing there, looking as if the

Facing page A formroom at Westminster School in 1846

town belonged to them, and nodding in a familiar manner to the coachman, as if any one of them would be equal to getting on the box, and working the team down street as well as he.'

Clarendon Commission (*1864*) In 1864 a Royal Commission on the Public Schools decided that too much time was still spent on learning classical languages, but: 'We are satisfied, on the whole both that it (the public school system) has been eminently successful, and that it has been greatly improved during the last thirty or forty years, partly by causes of a general kind, partly by the personal influence and exertions of Dr Arnold and other great schoolmasters ...

'The old roughness in manners has in great measure disappeared, and with it the petty tyranny and thoughtless cruelty which were formerly too common, and which used indeed to be thought inseparable from the life of a public school (62).'

Academies for young ladies For the daughters of middle class families aspiring to become 'ladies' a number of boarding schools were available. Despite the grand claims and lavish prospectuses issued by their principals, the education which they provided was usually very superficial. Even in many of the better-run schools, conditions were harsh, the food poor, and the morals low. Charlotte Bronte's *Jane Eyre* (1847) paints a picture of one such academy: 'The night passed rapidly ... When I again unclosed my eyes, a loud bell was ringing: the girls were up and dressing; day had not yet begun to dawn, and a rushlight or two burnt in the room. I too rose reluctantly; it was bitter cold, and I dressed as well as I could for shivering, and washed when there was a basin at liberty, which did not occur soon, as there was but one basin to six girls, on the stands down the middle of the room.'

Later, at breakfast: 'Ravenous, and now very faint, I devoured a spoonful or two of my portion without thinking of its taste; but the first edge of hunger blunted, I perceived I had got in hand a nauseous mess: burnt porridge is almost as bad as rotten potatoes.

'The spoons were moved slowly: I saw each girl taste her food and try to swallow it; but in most cases the effort was soon relinquished. Breakfast was over, and none had breakfasted. Thanks being returned for what we had not got, and a second hymn chanted, the refectory was evacuated for the schoolroom.'

For Rosa Bud, a pupil at the Nuns' House Ladies' Seminary

invented by Dickens, life was less severe. Miss Twinkleton, the Principal, was kind-hearted and genteel. Rosa was surprised to discover, however, that when Miss Twinkleton read aloud to her: 'She cut the love-scenes, interpolated passages in praise of female celibacy, and was guilty of other glaring pious frauds (63).'

Girls who attended these schools often became governesses in upper-class homes. A character of Thackeray's, Miss Pinkerton of The Mall, Chiswick, was asked to find one for Lady Fuddleston, and suggested two candidates: 'Either of these young ladies is perfectly qualified to instruct in Greek, Latin, and the rudiments of Hebrew; in mathematics and history, in Spanish, French, Italian, and geography; in music, vocal and instrumental; in dancing, without the aid of a master; and in the elements of natural sciences. *Governesses*

'In the use of the globes both are proficients. In addition to these, Miss Tuffin ... can instruct in the Syriac language, and the elements of Constitutional law. But as she is only eighteen years of age, and of exceedingly pleasing personal appearance, perhaps this young lady may be objectionable in Sir Huddleston Fuddleston's family.

'Miss Letitia Jawky, on the other hand, is not personally well-favoured. She is twenty-nine; her face is much pitted with the smallpox. She has a halt in her gait, red hair, and a trifling obliquity of vision. Both ladies are endowed with every moral and religious virtue. (64)'

Dickens was the first English novelist in whose books children play the main parts. Throughout his life he was deeply interested in the welfare of the young. He regularly visited schools: before writing *Nicholas Nickleby* he made several excursions to see those in Yorkshire. Altogether, he features over thirty schools in his stories. Here is one: 'The child looked round the room as she took her seat. There were a couple of forms [benches], notched and cut and inked all over; a small deal desk perched on four legs, at which no doubt the master sat; a few dog's-eared books upon a high shelf; and beside them a motley collection of peg-tops, balls, kites, fishing-lines, marbles, half-eaten apples, and other confiscated property of idle urchins. *Dickens and education*

'Displayed on hooks upon the wall in all their terrors were the cane and ruler; and near them, on a shelf of its own, the dunce's cap, made of old newspapers and decorated with glaring wafers of the largest size. But, the great ornaments of the walls were certain moral sentences fairly copied in good round text and well-worked sums in simple addition and multiplication (65).'

Copperfield at school When David Copperfield went to school, he was very soon in trouble:

'Suddenly I came upon a pasteboard placard, beautifully written, which was lying on the desk, and bore these words—"Take care of him. He bites."

'I got upon the desk immediately, apprehensive of at least a great dog underneath. But, though I looked all round with anxious eyes, I could see nothing of him. I was still engaged in peering about, when Mr Mell came back, and asked me what I did up there.

"I beg your pardon, sir," says I, "if you please, I'm looking for the dog."

"Dog?" says he. "What dog?"

"Isn't it a dog, sir?"

"Isn't what a dog?"

"That's to be taken care of, sir; that bites."

"No, Copperfield," says he gravely, "that's not a dog. That's a boy. My instructions are, Copperfield, to put this placard on your back. I am sorry to make such a beginning with you, but I must do it." (66)'

'Nicholas Nickleby' Nicholas Nickleby felt great apprehension about going to his new school: '"Is it much further to Dotheboys Hall, sir?" asked Nicholas.

"About three miles from here," replied Squeers. "But you needn't call it a Hall down here."

'Nicholas coughed, as if he would like to know why.

"The fact is, it ain't a Hall," observed Squeers drily.

"Oh, indeed?" said Nicholas, whom this piece of intelligence much astonished.

"No," replied Squeers. "We call it a Hall up in London, because it sounds better, but they don't know it by that name in these parts ..." ... they reached their journey's end.

"Jump out," said Squeers. "Hallo there! come and put this horse up. Be quick, will you."

'While the schoolmaster was uttering these and other impatient cries, Nicholas had time to observe that the school was a long cold-looking house, one storey high, with a few straggling outbuildings behind, and a barn and a stable adjoining ...

'A host of unpleasant misgivings, which had been crowding upon Nicholas during the whole journey, thronged into his mind with redoubled force (67).'

Such were the schools of Dickens' day, for the most part feared, criticised and ridiculed. For the first time, however, people were coming to realise the social importance of education in the life of the nation. Government investigations combined with the stirring of public conscience, paved the way for the reforms in the educational system which were to come after Dickens' death.

5 *Crime and Punishment*

THE JUDICIAL system of Dickens' day was barbarous and out-moded. In the early 1800s, law enforcement was most ineffective and penalties—for those who were caught—correspondingly severe. Crimes were classified as felonies or misdemeanours. Misdemeanours were trivial offences, minor breaches of the peace such as drunkenness or insulting behaviour. Felonies, however, covered everything from theft to murder, and all such offences were punishable with hanging. A petty pickpocket had as much to fear as an assassin: 'as well be hung for a sheep as a lamb,' as the saying went. *Barbarous system*

All suspected persons were thrown into prison to await trial at the next assizes or sessions. Those who came off worst were those imprisoned in the county jails, where they might have to wait three or four months for the assize to come to town. Gaolers had a great reputation for violence and corruption, which a well-off prisoner could allay by weekly payments. Despite the maxim 'innocent until proved guilty', no discrimination was made between prisoners awaiting trial and those serving sentences. They shared the same conditions in prison, and in those days no prisoner had any right to food and drink from the authorities. With the aid of relatives or friends he had to make do as best he could. Many were forced to take their families with them into prison. *Prisons*

London had many prisons, the most famous of which included the Bridewell, the Fleet, and the two Compters for use by the Sheriffs of London. But the most famous of all was Newgate Prison. Dickens wrote in *Nicholas Nickleby* (1839): 'There, at the very core of London, in the heart of its business and animation, in the

65

Scenes at Newgate Prison. *Top left* a prisoner consults his attorney, *top right* the condemned cell, *below left* the flogging-box and *below right* prisoners working

D

midst of a whirl of noise and motion: stemming as it were the giant currents of life that flow ceaselessly on from different quarters and meet beneath its walls: stands Newgate.'

Debtors   As well as people awaiting trial at the Old Bailey, and prisoners serving sentences, Newgate held many poor debtors. Perhaps no class of people suffered more unjustly under an antiquated regime. Although debt was a civil—not a criminal—offence, debtors often had to pay more dearly than criminals. A thief might at least be given a fixed prison term, of seven or ten years; but a debtor who could not repay a debt of a few shillings would spend the rest of his days in gaol, and once in gaol, he probably had no means of earning money to repay the debt. Abuses of the system by the ruthless were quite notorious. Dishonest statements often led to innocent people losing their freedom.

Inspectors   Criticism of the prisons' whole system is given in the First Report of the Prison Inspectorate: 'We deem it our duty to mark the evils of the system, now for a long period in disastrous operation in the gaol of Newgate ... The Association of Prisoners of all ages, and of every shade of guilt, in one indiscriminate mass, is a frightful feature of the system which prevails here; the first in magnitude, and the most pernicious in effect ... Another feature ... is the utter absence of all employment for the prisoners.'

The object of Newgate and other prisons was to make their inmates' stay 'inside' as unpleasant as possible. Tread-wheels were used in many prisons: 'To the present century belongs ... the high philosophic honour of having contrived an apparatus like the tread-wheel.' This 'combines the double oral absurdity of rendering prison labour not only more than usually irksome, but also more than usually profitless.'

We 'seek to impress lazy men with a sense of beauty and value of industry, by the invention of an instrument which is especially adapted to render labour inordinately repulsive, by making it inordinately useless (68).' Reformers found no merit in this.

In many prisons the inmates were forbidden even to speak: 'From the recent introduction of silence into some prisons I have not yet been able to trace a single instance of mischievous con-
Silent prisons   sequences. My conversations with prisoners, officers, surgeons, chaplains and magistrates, have not led to the discovery of any

Pentonville, 1867, a model prison with separate cells

case in which disease, either of body or of mind, has been affirmed by any party to have grown out of this mode of discipline.

'The experiment, it is true, has not yet been practised for a long period; but I am bound to add, that all the persons most conversant with the interior of prisons ... pronounce decidedly in its favour, and entertain an expectation of its probable efficacy in increasing the repugnance of incarceration (69).' Such were the words of one of the earliest official prison reports.

In 1842, Pentonville, the first of several new prisons, was opened. It was one of the first to introduce the novelty of separate cells: 'Now let us enter the cell. Well, really it has anything but a repulsive appearance ... It is sufficiently large being thirteen feet long, seven broad, and nine high. It is admirably ventilated, on the newest scientific principle, and by means of warm air is kept at an even and agreeable temperature. It has even the luxuries of a water-closet, and of an unlimited supply of warm and cold water.'

A model prison

Beds are 'clean and good; the food is also good, and plentiful in supply ... Light work is to be had also for amusement and to vary the routine ... At regular intervals the prisoner goes to chapel to hear the gospel; and to school, where competent masters are waiting to offer their services to instruct him (70).'

Crime was one of the gravest social problems in Dickens's day and played an important part in his novels. The melodrama of this other world fascinated him, as it shocked others who refused to believe such a picture could be true.

He wrote, 'the merry old gentleman and the two boys played at a very curious and uncommon game, which was performed in this way. The merry old gentleman, placing a snuff-box in one pocket of his trousers, a note-case in the other, and a watch in his waist-coat pocket, with a guard-chain round his neck, and sticking a mock diamond pin in his shirt: buttoned his coat tight round him, and putting his spectacle-case and handkerchiefs in his pockets, trotted up and down the room with a stick, in imitation of the manner in which old gentlemen walk about the streets any hour of the day ... the two boys followed him closely about: getting out of his sight, so nimbly, every time he turned round, that it was impossible to follow their motions.

'At last, the Dodger trod upon his toes, or ran upon his boot accidentally, while Charley Bates stumbled up against him behind; and in that one moment they took from him, with the most extraordinary rapidity, snuff-box, note-case, watch-guard, chain, shirt-pin, pocket-handkerchief, even the spectacle-case. If the old gentleman felt a hand in any one of his pockets, he cried out where it was; and then the game began all over again (71).'

Although interested in crime, Dickens had little sympathy for the criminal. He favoured the continued use of the tread-wheel, defended the 'silent system' and thought that to spend money on model prisons like Pentonville was a useless waste: 'On the appointed day ... I repaired to the prison [Pentonville] where Mr Creakle was powerful. It was an immense and solid building, erected at a vast expense. I could not help thinking, as we approached the gate, what an uproar would have been made in the country, if any deluded man had proposed to spend one half the money it had cost, on the erection of an industrial school for the young, or a house of refuge for the deserving old ... After some conversation ... from which I might have supposed that there was nothing in the world to be legitimately taken into account but the supreme comfort of prisoners, at any expense, and nothing on the wide earth to be done outside prison-doors, we began our inspection (72).'

69

Facing page Crime flourished in surroundings like this, Field Lane, 1840

In his essay *The Ruffian* (1868) Dickens asked: 'Why is a notorious Thief and Ruffian ever left at large? He never turns his liberty to any account but violence and plunder, he never did a day's work out of gaol, he never will do a day's work out of gaol ... I demand to have the Ruffian kept out of my way, and out of the way of all decent people. I demand to have the Ruffian employed, perforce, in hewing wood and drawing water somewhere for the general service, instead of hewing at her Majesty's subjects, and drawing their watches out of their pockets.'

By the 1840s capital crimes had been reduced to murder, treason and offences against property which were accompanied by violence to the person. For a time Dickens campaigned for the abolition of the death penalty: 'I learn from the newspaper accounts of every execution, how Mr So-and-so, and Mr Somebody else, and Mr So-forth shook hands with the culprit, but I never find them shaking hands with the hangman. All kinds of attention and consideration are lavished on the one; but the other is universally avoided, like a pestilence.

'I want to know why so much sympathy is expended on the man who kills another in the vehemence of his own bad passions, and why the man who kills him in the name of the law is shunned and fled from? Is it because the murderer is going to die? Then by no means put him to death. Is it because the hangman executes a law, which, when they once come near it face to face, all men instinctively revolt from? Then by all means change it (73).'

Public executions were not stopped by law until 1868. These spectacles drew large crowds, who treated them as festive occasions. Dickens was disgusted by all this: 'I believe that a sight so inconceivably awful as the wickedness and levity of the immense crowd collected at that execution this morning could be imagined by no man, and could be presented in no heathen land under the sun. The horrors of the gibbet and of the crime which brought the wretched murderers to it faded in my mind before the atrocious bearing, looks, and language of the assembled spectators. When I came upon the scene at midnight, the shrillness of the cries and howls that were raised from time to time, denoting that they came from a concourse of boys and girls already assembled in the best places, made my blood run cold ...

THE EXECUTION OF
JAMES CLITHEROE,
Of St. Helen's, for the Murder of Mary Woods, this day.

Crowds attending a public execution

'When the two miserable creatures who attracted all this ghastly sight about them were turned quivering into the air, there was no more emotion, no more pity, no more thought that two immortal souls had gone to judgment, no more restraint in any of the previous obscenities, than if the name of Christ had never been heard in this world, and there were no belief among men but that they perished like the beasts.

'I have seen, habitually, some of the worst sources of general contamination and corruption in this country, and I think there are not many phases of London life that could surprise me. I am solemnly convinced that nothing that ingenuity could devise to be done in this city, in the same compass of time, could work such ruin as one public execution, and I stand astounded and appalled by the wickedness it exhibits. I do not believe that any community can prosper where such a scene of horror and demoralisation as was enacted this morning outside Horsemonger Lane Gaol is presented at the very doors of good citizens, and is passed by unknown or forgotten (74).'

Times were changing. One remembers that only two generations before, in 1783, Dr Johnson had grumbled that the great procession of the condemned to Tyburn was abolished. Johnson had complained, 'The public was gratified by a procession, the criminal was supported by it. Why is all this to be swept away?'

Juvenile offenders

Mary Carpenter wrote anxiously of the rise in juvenile offences: 'It appears from parliamentary returns and other authentic documents, that during the present century the number of commitments and convictions has increased in this country greatly beyond the increase of population ... the number of juvenile criminals has increased in a greater degree than even the mass of criminals at large (75).'

Reformers like Mary Carpenter believed that, if this increase was to be checked, something had to be done about those children, 'who have not yet fallen into actual crime, but who are almost certain from their ignorance, destitution, and the circumstances in which they are growing up, to do so, if a helping hand be not extended to raise them [as well as to those] who have already received the prison brand, or if the mark has not been yet visibly set upon them, are notoriously living by plunder (76).'

What could be done? In December 1851 a Conference was held at Birmingham to consider: 'The Condition and Treatment of the "Perishing and Dangerous" Classes of Children and Juvenile Offenders, with a view of procuring such Legislative Enactments as may produce a beneficial change in their actual condition and their prospects ... Education, including both instruction and training, is the only means of effecting any material diminution of juvenile crime (77).'

Special schools

The Conference voted that, for the first class of children, there should be special schools to which their parents would have to send them. For the second class, members favoured the setting-up of 'reformatory schools'. Magistrates could send juvenile offenders here, instead of to prison.

Mary Carpenter wrote: 'It is no longer a subject for doubt that the old and unreformed prisons, where classification was impossible, where the young child charged with his first offence was exposed to the contaminating influence of the experienced felons, were schools of vice to the juvenile offenders, which it was nearly impossible that any could enter without being ruined for life.

'Though numbers of new prisons have been built on an improved plan, and others altered so as to secure some degree of separation among the prisoners, yet the Select Committee of the House of Commons on Prison Discipline, in July 1850, "deem it their duty to state that several prisons are still in a very unsatisfactory condition; and that proper punishment, separation, or reformation in them is nearly impossible".'

She gave an example: 'In Newgate, for instance, the actual construction of the prison renders separation impracticable; there were, The Governor reports ... "400 boys under 16 out of 3,000 annually in gaol"; there is an attempt to separate the tried and untried juvenile prisoners who are kept distinct from the adults in a school yard. There is no means of preventing contamination and communication between the prisoners at night, when from 6 to 15 are in each ward; in the winter the wards are locked without light at 5, and unlocked at 7, consequently 14 hours out of the 24 the prisoners are in darkness, without supervision (78).'

During the 1850s a number of reformatory schools were established. A new climate was felt. For the first time, the authorities were beginning to recognise crime as a social problem, the solutions to which lay in their own hands.

73

6 Speeding Ahead

DURING HIS lifetime, Dickens witnessed great changes in transport, which affected town and countryside alike. Proprietors of road transport, railways and canals competed fiercely with each other for a stake in commerce, and their very competitiveness helped industrial change by speeding up communications and the movement of goods. Many passions were aroused, involving farmers, railwaymen, travellers, industrialists, 'navvies', and all those whose lives were revolutionised in these momentous times. In transport, industry, and agriculture, Britain was 'speeding ahead', and there were many casualties *en route*.

Coaching

Let us look through the eyes of contemporaries, and begin with Dickens' picture of a noisy coaching yard: 'The mail itself goes on to the coach-office in due course, and the passengers who are going out by the early coach stare with astonishment at the passengers who are coming in by the early coach, who look blue and dismal ... The coach-office is all alive, and the coaches which are just going out, are surrounded by the usual crowd of Jews and nondescripts, who seem to consider, Heaven knows why, that it is quite impossible any man can mount a coach without requiring at least sixpenny-worth of oranges, a penknife, a pocket-book, a last year's annual, a pencil-case, a piece of sponge, and a series of caricatures (79).'

When Dickens described this early morning scene at one of London's coach-offices, the great era of the stage-coach was already at an end.

Travelling by coach could be an uncomfortable experience: 'The night was not so pleasant as the evening, for it got chilly; and

Facing page London coaching scenes, *above* the West Country mails at the Gloucester coffee house, Piccadilly, *below* the Cambridge Telegraph departing from Fetter Lane

being put between two gentlemen ... to prevent my tumbling off the coach, I was nearly smothered by their falling asleep and completely blocking me up ... Opposite me was an elderly lady in a great fur cloak, who ... had a basket with her, and she hadn't known what to do with it, for a long time, until she found that, on account of my legs being short, it could go underneath me. It cramped and hurt me so that it made me miserable; but if I moved in the least ... she gave me the cruellest poke with her foot.' This picture was painted by Dickens in *David Copperfield* (1850).

Petition to Parliament Coaching companies found it more and more difficult to compete with new forms of transport. Unfair taxation, they complained, took their living away from them:

'To the Honourable the COMMONS ... in Parliament assembled.

'Your petitioners beg to lay before your Honourable House the following statements in the hope, that you may see fit to recommend a relief from the burthens they at present experience:

'That the interests of your petitioners have, for a long time, suffered by the number of steam vessels, running parallel to the east line of coast; and, while other branches of trade have been on the increase, that of your petitioners has been on the decline ...

'During the past year, the great increase, in number and magnitude, of steam packets, produced a competition among them, and consequent lowering of fares, which operated very seriously on your petitioners, whose conveyances, from the nature of their business, would not admit temporary suspension ...

'That your petitioners have endeavoured to compete with steam, by a great reduction of their fares, which they found unavailing; and they find, in practice, that, owing to the improvements in steam navigation, and the ease, certainty, and economy it accomplishes, many persons visiting the north find it preferable to a conveyance by land ...

'Your petitioners submit, that while coaching and posting were the only modes of communication, they were fair objects of taxation ...

'They would further urge the consideration of their situation, in consequence of the prospect before them, of their business being, in many districts, superseded by railways, and themselves obliged to seek other modes of employment (80).'

But the railways were here to stay. The very fact that they were putting coach proprietors out of business argued their value, and by and large Parliament did little to hold them back. Many private Acts of Parliament were passed, setting up railways, and giving them statutory power to forge their way through farmland. Britain's railway system grew at a rapid rate: in 1840 there were less than 2,000 miles of track; by 1870 the mileage exceeded 15,000.

Many people were alarmed by this development, fearing that it would disturb their way of life:

> 'Is then no nook of English ground secure
> From rash assault? Schemes of retirement sown
> In youth, and 'mid the busy world kept pure
> As when their earliest flowers of hope were blown,
> Must perish; how can they this blight endure?'

(From William Wordsworth, *On the projected Kendal and Winder-mere Railway*, 1844.)

Benjamin Disraeli reflected opinion in his book *Sybil* (1845):

'"You came by the railroad?" inquired Lord de Mowbray mournfully, of Lady Marney.

"From Marham; about ten miles from us," replied her ladyship.

"A great revolution!"

"Isn't it?"

"I fear it has a very dangerous tendency to equality," said his lordship, shaking his head; "I suppose Lord Marney gives them all the opposition in his power."

"There is nobody so violent against railroads as George," said Lady Marney; "I cannot tell you what he does not do! He organised the whole division against the Marham line!"

"I rather counted on him," said Lord de Mowbray, "to assist me in resisting this joint branch here; but I was surprised to learn he had consented."

"Not until the compensation was settled," innocently remarked Lady Marney: "George never opposes them after that. He gave up all opposition to the Marham line when they agreed to his terms."

"And yet," said Lord de Mowbray, "I think if Lord Marney would take a different view of the case and look to the moral consequences, he would hesitate. Equality, Lady Marney, equality

is not our métier. If we nobles do not make a stand against the levelling spirit of the age, I am at a loss to know who will fight the battle. You may depend upon it that these railroads are very dangerous things."

"I have no doubt of it. I suppose you have heard of Lady Vanilla's trip from Birmingham? Have you not, indeed! She came up with Lady Laura, and two of the most gentlemanlike men sitting opposite her; never met, she says, two more intelligent men. She begged one of them at Wolverhampton to change seats with her, and he was most politely willing to comply with her wishes, only it was necessary that his companion should move at the same time, for they were chained together! Two gentlemen, sent to town for picking a pocket at Shrewsbury races."

"A countess and a felon! So much for public conveyances," said Lord Mowbray, "but Lady Vanilla is one of those who will talk with everybody."'

In her classic *Middlemarch* (1872), George Eliot's characters echoed these sentiments: *George Eliot*

'"But some say this country's seen its best days, and the sign is as it's being over run with these fellows trampling right and left and wanting to cut it up into railways; and all for the big traffic to swallow up the little, so as there sha'n't be a team left on the land, nor a whip to crack."

"I'll crack *my* whip about their ear'n, afore they bring it to that though," said Hiram.'

John Ruskin, however, drew a powerfully romantic picture of railways: 'And along the iron veins that traverse the frame of our *A penny a mile* country, beat and flow the fiery pulses of its exertions, hotter and faster every hour. All vitality is concentrated through those throbbing arteries into the central cities (81).'

Despite everything said against them, the railways meant faster travel. Parliament now made sure it was available for those who could only afford a penny a mile: 'Companies [must] provide upon such new Lines of Railway, as a *minimum* of third-class accommodation, one Train at least each way on every week-day, by which there shall be the ordinary stations, in carriages provided with seats and protected from the weather, at a speed not less than 12 miles an hour including stoppages, and at fares not exceeding a penny

79

Facing page The entrance to the railway tunnel at Clerkenwell pictured in 1868

per mile; each Passenger by such Train being allowed not exceeding 56 lbs of luggage without extra charge, and extra luggage being charged by weight at a rate not exceeding the lowest charge by other Trains: Children under Three years being conveyed without extra charge; and Children from Three to Twelve years at half-price (82).'

George Hudson
At first the railways were run by scores of small local companies, each of which owned a short stretch of track. This was an uneconomic arrangement and before long companies began to amalgamate to share their costs. George Hudson played a prominent part in this complicated business and for a time was 'uncrowned king' of Britain's railways:

'In 1844 [Hudson's] influence extended seventy-six miles over the York and North Midland; fifty-one miles over the Hull and Selby and Leeds and Selby; over the North Midland, Midland Counties and another (the Birmingham and Derby Junction), one hundred and seventy-eight miles; over the Newcastle and Darlington, and the Great North of England, one hundred and eleven miles; while over the Sheffield and Rotherham, the York and Scarborough, the North British, Whitby and Pickering, it affected nearly six hundred more, making a total of 1,016 miles, all of which were successful in developing traffic, and equally successful in paying good dividends (83).'

One witness, giving evidence to a Parliamentary Committee, declared that amalgamation had brought higher fares: 'In the earlier history of the so-called competing lines a very considerable temporary diminution took place in the fares and freights to the public, but in a very short time those lines coalesced and combined, and the result has been, I think, in almost every instance where the game has been played out, I may say in every instance, to raise the rates to a higher standard than they were at before the competition commenced (84).'

Agricultural workers
One must remember, however, that in the 1840s, Britain was still predominantly a rural nation, with at least half the population working on the land. The enclosure of arable land, which was now almost complete, had resulted in the drift of some countrymen to the towns. Many others, having lost their smallholdings, had become labourers.

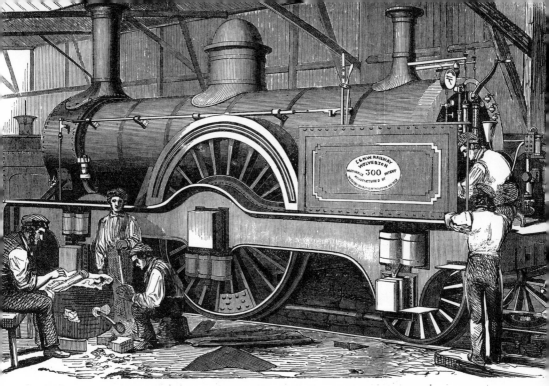

Building an express engine for the London and North-Western Railway in 1852

Life was not easy for the labourer's family and all its members had to work. Let us look at an extract from the Report of the Commission on Employment of Women and Children in Agriculture, made to Parliament in 1843. This statement was taken down from a woman:

'I began to work in the fields when I was quite a girl. I helped my father to bind up the corn when he was reaping. I have reaped myself as much as half an acre a day, and tied it up. I and another have reaped an acre a day between us. In harvest I have worked nearly night and day, at the time that I had four or five children. At other times of the year I have worked at all kinds of things in the fields, turnip-hoeing, hay-making and stone-picking. At hay-making and other times I went out at six in the morning, and got home at six in the evening; hours are earlier and later at harvest. At hay-time and harvest I am paid better than at other times. When a girl I got 2s a week; afterwards 8d a day.'

Squatters, like 'Farmer' Ives—a character in *Tom Brown's* *Enclosures*
Schooldays (1857)—might still live on common land or waste,

but their future was threatened by enclosure: 'Why he was called "farmer" I cannot say, unless it be that he was the owner of a cow, a pig or two, and some poultry, which he maintained on about an acre of land inclosed from the middle of a wild common, on which probably his father had squatted before lords of manors looked as keenly after their rights as they do now. Here he had lived no one knew how long, a solitary man. It was often rumoured that he was to be turned out and his cottage pulled down, but somehow it never came to pass; and his pigs and cow went grazing on the common, and his geese hissed at the passing children and at the heels of the horse of my lord's steward, who often rode by with a covetous eye on the inclosure still unmolested (85).'

Farming makes progress The repeal of the Corn Laws in 1846—supposed to have protected farmers—ushered in a period of prosperity for British agriculture previously unknown. Many were surprised by this. Outdated eighteenth century methods were discarded and replaced by more efficient techniques. A wide range of farming machinery was brought into use. Many farmers added guano and phosphates to their soil to make it more fertile. Dairying underwent a big expansion, the herds now being fed on root crops during the winter months.

James Caird writes in his book on English agriculture, published in the 1850s: 'The safe course for the English agriculturalist is to endeavour, by increasing his livestock, to render himself less dependent on corn, while he at the same time enriches his farm by their manure, and is thus enabled to grow heavier crops at less comparative cost.'

'The great aim in the culture of the farm,' he added, 'is the early preparation of the land intended for the turnip crop; to this all other work is postponed after the corn crops have been secured in autumn. The stubbles are then stirred in one direction by Biddle's "scarifier", the sharp-pointed tines being used in this operation, and the ground torn up to a depth of five or six inches. After the field has been gone over once, the "scarifier" is fitted with the broadshare tines, and made to cross the former stirring at right angles, thus tearing the ground to pieces, and disengaging the stubbles and roots of weeds and twitch, which are drawn together on the surface with the harrows, then gathered by the horse-rake and laid in a heap ...

The engine in agriculture, a threshing and stocking machine of the 1860s

'The land, now thoroughly pulverised, is ploughed with a clean deep furrow, and in that state is left exposed to the influence of the weather till spring, when it receives one furrow more, and is found in fine condition ... The swedes are sown on the ridge, twenty-eight to thirty inches apart, eight loads of well-rotted farmyard dung and 1½ cwt of guano per acre being previously applied and covered in on the weakest land ... On the better land 14 tons of dung and 1½ cwt of guano per acre are applied (86).'

Many farmers dreaded the railways cutting across their meadows. *Railways and* The noise frightened livestock, and sparks were a fire risk. Yet the *farmers* coming of the railway was a great benefit to the farmer. New markets in the towns were opened to his products; he could get quicker delivery of machinery, pipes, fertilisers, and other goods. The movement of animals was also made easier; it was no longer necessary to drive livestock long journeys to market.

James Caird explained, before the railway in Norfolk: 'Cattle and sheep for the Smithfield Monday market had to leave their homes on the previous Wednesday or Thursday week. Such a long drift, particularly in hot weather, caused a great waste of meat. The heavy stall-fed cattle of East Norfolk suffered severely. The average loss on such bullocks was considered to be 4 stones of 14 lb, while the best yearling sheep are proved to have lost 6 lb of mutton and 4 lb of tallow ... Stock now leave on Saturday and are in the salesmen's layers that evening, fresh for the metropolitan market on Monday morning (87).'

The Great Exhibition (1851) Britain's industry and trade were also entering a boom period. The new prosperity was symbolised by the Great Exhibition which opened in Hyde Park on 1 May 1851. Housed in the Crystal Palace, which was specially built for the occasion, it was a gigantic display 'of the Works and Industries of all Nations'.

Queen Victoria took a great interest, for her husband Albert had helped to plan the event. She wrote in her Diary on 1 May 1851: 'This day is one of the greatest and most glorious days of our lives, with which to my pride and joy, the name of my dearly beloved Albert is for ever associated! It is a day which makes my heart swell with thankfulness ...

'The park presented a wonderful spectacle, crowds streaming through it—carriages and troops passing, quite like the Coronation and for *me* the same anxiety. At a $\frac{1}{2}$p. eleven the whole procession of nine state carriages was set in motion ... The Green Park and Hyde Park were one mass of densely crowded human beings, in the highest good humour and most enthusiastic. I never saw Hyde Park look as it did, being filled with crowds as far as the eye could reach ... the sun shone and gleamed upon the gigantic edifice, upon which the flags of every nation were flying.'

'Magnificent spectacles' The next day *The Times* declared: 'There was yesterday witnessed a sight the like of which has never happened before, and which, in the nature of things, can never be repeated. They who were so fortunate as to see it hardly knew what most to admire, or in what form to clothe the sense of wonder, and even of mystery, which struggled within them. The edifice, the treasures of nature and art collected therein, the assemblage, and the solemnity of the occasion, all conspired to suggest something even more than sense could scan or imagination attain.'

Six million visitors The western part of the Crystal Palace was given over to British exhibits, the eastern half to those from other countries: 'In the midst is seen the Fountain of Glass; behind it, and also in groups near the south entrance, are beautiful tropical plants, sheltered by the elm trees which rise above them; and above all springs the light and elegant arch of the wonderful Transept. The glitter of the falling waters in the gleaming light which pours down in this part of the building, and the artistic arrangement of the groups of objects of art and industry in the immediate neighbourhood of the Transept, makes this a peculiarly attractive part of this immense structure (88).'

The six million visitors to the Crystal Palace during the summer

The *Great Eastern* being towed to Cork after gales

of 1851 went away delighted with what they had seen. Their enthusiasm contrasted sharply with the misgivings which many had expressed before the opening: 'The whole of Hyde Park, and we venture to predict, the whole of Kensington Gardens, will be turned into the bivouac of all the vagabonds of London so long as the Exhibition shall continue. The annoyance inflicted upon the neighbourhood will be indescribable (89).'

Charles Dickens referred to the criticisms of the Crystal Palace when, at a London dinner on 9 June 1851, he rose to propose the health of Joseph Paxton, who had designed the building. The Crystal Palace, he declared, 'ought to have fallen down, but it had refused to do so. We were told that the glass ought to have been all broken, the gutters all choked up, and the building flooded, and that the roof and sides ought to have blown away; in short, that everything ought to have done what everything obstinately per-

Joseph Paxton

sisted in not doing. Earth, air, fire and water all appear to have conspired together in Mr Paxton's favour—all had conspired to one result, which, when the present generation was in dust, would be an enduring temple to his honour, and to the energy, the talent, and the resources of Englishmen.'

The Exhibition was a huge success. Large profits were made, and these were used to set up a permanent centre at South Kensington to promote science and the arts: 'This is the only country which has neither supplied (in any practical form) Scientific or Artistic instruction to its industrial population; nor, for men of Science and Art, a centre of learning and of exchange of the results of their work ...

'Yet this country, as the centre of commerce and industry of the world, would seem to require, more than any other, to have these needs supplied. And the Great Exhibition of last year has, in its results, convinced us that, unless they be speedily organised, this country will run serious risk of losing that foremost position which now makes its strength and its boast (90).' Such was the warning in an official report.

Free trade   On 23 November 1852, Parliament attributed national progress to the idea of 'free trade': 'That it is the opinion of this House that the improved condition of the country, and especially of the industrious classes is mainly the result of recent legislation, which has established the principle of unrestricted competition and abolished taxes imposed for the purposes of protection, and has thereby diminished the cost and increased the abundance of the principal articles of food to the people.

'That it is the opinion of this House that that policy firmly maintained and prudently extended, will best enable the industry of the country to bear its burdens, and will thereby most surely promote the welfare and contentment of the people.'

This resolution, introduced by Lord Palmerston into the House of Commons, was passed by 468 votes to 43. Members of Parliament may have overestimated the effects of the free trade measures which had been taken, but no one could deny that the nation was enjoying a growing prosperity.

'Workshop of   Britain had become 'the workshop of the world', and for a
the World'   quarter of a century she was to remain the major exporter of

The Great Exhibition at Crystal Palace in 1851

machinery and manufactured goods: 'Thirty years ago England had almost a monopoly of the manufacturing industries of the world; she produced everything in excess of her consumption, other nations comparatively nothing. The world was obliged to buy from her, because it could not buy anywhere else (91).'

As in past centuries, British prosperity went hand-in-hand with maritime power, and the existence of a large merchant navy which exported British manufactured goods to every corner of the globe. For this reason, the Victorians were as proud of being an island race as 'workshop of the world', and it is to these aspects which we will now turn.

7 A Seafaring Nation

THE FIRST crossing of the Atlantic under steam power alone was made in 1838. Two years later *Britannia*, a wooden vessel built on the Clyde, became the first steamship to carry mail from this country to North America. Sailing between Liverpool and Boston, it took about fifteen days to complete a crossing, and was a marvel to contemporaries. *Crossing the Atlantic*

Dickens himself visited America in 1841, voyaging aboard the *Britannia*. Later he wrote about his experiences: 'I opened the door of, and put my head into, a "state-room" on board the *Britannia* steam-packet, twelve hundred tons burthen per register, bound for Halifax and Boston, and carrying Her Majesty's mails ...

'Before descending into the bowels of the ship, we had passed from the deck into a long narrow apartment, not unlike a gigantic hearse with windows in the sides; having at the upper end a melancholy stove, at which three or four chilly stewards were warming their hands; while on either side, extending down its whole dreary length, was a long, long table, over each of which a rack, fixed to the low roof, and stuck full of drinking-glasses, and cruet-stands, hinted dismally at rolling seas and heavy weather.'

Then at midnight, 'we shipped a sea which forced its way through the skylights, burst open the doors above, and came raging and roaring down into the ladies' cabin, to the unspeakable consternation of my wife and a little Scotch lady—who, by the way, had previously sent a message to the captain by the stewardess, requesting him with her compliments, to have a steel conductor immediately attached to the top of every mast, and to the chimney, in order that the ship might not be struck by lightning (92).' In *Eothen* *Rough seas*

The Grand Saloon of the *Great Eastern* during gales

'Dockland' (1845) A. W. Kinglake wrote that 'The ships of the English swarm like flies.' The port of London became busier and still busier as the volume of shipping rose during the middle years of the century. Dickens wrote:

'In some of the vessels at anchor all hands were busily engaged in coiling ropes, spreading out sails to dry, taking in or discharging their cargoes; in others, no life was visible but two or three tarry boys, and perhaps a barking dog running to and fro upon the deck or scrambling up to look over the side and bark the louder for the view.

'Coming slowly on through the forests of masts, was a great steam ship, beating the water in short impatient strokes with her heavy paddles, as though she wanted room to breathe, and advancing in her huge bulk like a sea monster among the minnows of the Thames. On either hand, were long black tiers of colliers; between them, vessels slowly working out of harbour with sails glistening in the sun, and creaking noise on board, re-echoed from a hundred quarters (93).'

The Thames In his *Notes on England* (1872), H. A. Taine painted a vivid picture of the Thames: 'The Thames is a mile broad, and is but a populous street of vessels, a winding work-yard. Steamboats, sailing vessels, ascend and descend, come to anchor in groups of two, three, ten, then in long files, then in dense rows; there are five or six thousand of them at anchor. On the right, the docks, like so many intricate, maritime streets, disgorge or store up the vessels.

'If you get on a height, you see vessels in the distance by hundreds and thousands, fixed as if on the land; their masts in a line, their slender rigging, make a spider-web which girdles the horizon. Yet on the river itself, to the west, we see an inextricable forest of masts, yards, and cables; the ships are unloading, fastened to one another, mingled with chimneys, among the pulleys of the store-houses, cranes, capstans, and all the implements of the vast and ceaseless toil.

'A foggy smoke, penetrated by the sun, wraps them in its russet veil; it is the heavy and smoky air of a great hot-house; soil and man, light and air, all is transformed by work. If you enter one of these docks, the impression will be yet more overwhelming: each resembles a town; always ships, still more ships, in a line, showing their heads; their hollowed sides, their copper chests, like monstrous fishes under the breastplate of scales. When we descend below, we see that this breastplate is fifty feet high; many are of three thousand or four thousand tons. Long clippers of three hundred feet are on the point of sailing for Australia, Ceylon, America.'

The Thames was a great haunt of thieves and robbers who prowled among the docked ships for cargo pickings, and a special police force had to be created. Dickens described it: 'There are, in the Thames Police Force, whose district extends from Battersea to Barking Creek, ninety-eight men, eight duty boats, and two supervision boats ... these go about so silently and lie in wait in such dark places, and so seem to be nowhere, and so may be anywhere, that they have gradually become a police of prevention, keeping the river almost clear of any great crimes (94).' *Thames police*

Viewed as a highway for shipping, the river presented a romantic picture. Many Londoners, however, saw it in a different light: for them it was little better than an open sewer. *Punch* (26 June 1858) was among those demanding action to purify its waters: *'Punch' and the Thames*

> Piff, piff-piff, piff, piff-piff!
> Thou noisome Thames River,
> When I thy stench sniff, piff!
> I shudder and shiver.
> Piff, piff-piff! how horrid
> Is thy filth, thick as cream,
> Baked by Summer's sun torrid,
> It reeks with foul steam!
>
> Piff, piff-piff! what fetor!
> Than a sewer no sweeter,
> Piff, piff! thou art meeter
> To spread o'er the field,
> Where the grass and the wheat are
> Rich harvests to yield,
> Than piff-piff! by paddle
> Or oar to be stirred;
> Piff-piff! than eggs addle
> Thou art worse, on my word!

As *Punch* remarked, 'The battle is as to who shall pay for the

91

Overleaf The hustle and bustle on London Bridge towards the end of Dickens' life

purification of the.Thames. The country objects, and we are afraid,
that some fine pestilential morning, Father Thames will make a
forcible appeal to the feelings of Englishmen, and throw himself
regularly upon the country in the shape of Cholera. It is said that
the sewage of the Thames is a sure, safe, and tid(e)y fortune, but
apparently no one likes to draw upon its banks (95).'

> O Faraday, of Chemists first,
> The Thames we have to clear,
> The Thames, with which we slake our thirst
> In water, or in beer.
> To take its foulness out to sea
> Will cost us deuce knows what:
> Now in this strait can Chemistry
> Afford us help, or not?

(*Punch*, 31 July 1858.)

Thames Dockland was a major shipbuilding centre. In 1858 the
Leviathan was under construction at Millwall. Renamed the *Great
Eastern*, she was the largest steamship to be built during the century.

Punch doubted the usefulness of such a vessel:

'What to do with the *Leviathan*: Many ingenious contrivances
have been suggested, but we like our own recommendation the
best. We propose that she be maintained as a kind of sewer-vessel,
for the purification of the Metropolis. Let the whole of the sewage
of this dirty London be emptied into her many holds; and, when all
of them are full, let her sail with the cargo right out to sea, and
discharge it in the middle of the ocean, where no human nostrils
are likely to be offended with it … In our opinion, the *Leviathan*
would make a first-rate floating sewer (96).'

As one can see, if experiments and progress were made, it was
never without much noisy protest and ribald criticism. Yet progress
was made: the introduction of steam power, and the building of
larger and faster ships—first with iron and then with steel—played
a vital role in increasing Britain's exports from £70 millions in 1850
to £200 millions by 1870, the twenty years which followed the repeal
of the Navigation Laws in 1849, and other protective legislation.

The great wealth of this sea-faring nation brought not only
prosperity, but a greater opportunity for leisure. As we shall see,
the Victorians showed much ingenuity in using it.

8 *Taking it Easy*

MID-VICTORIAN England, with its overcrowded towns, ragged *Fun at home*
children, cholera epidemics and bugs, does not sound an attractive
place in which to have lived. But, as Dickens himself shows in his
novels, there was a lighter side to life. Victorians knew how to
enjoy themselves in such free time as they had from work. In many
homes families amused themselves with dancing, music and games
as Dickens pictured in *A Christmas Carol* (1843):

'After tea, they had some music. For they were a musical family,
and knew what they were about, when they sung a Glee or a Catch,
I can assure you: especially Topper, who could growl away in the
bass like a good one, and never swell the large veins in his forehead,
or get red in the face. Scrooge's niece played well upon the harp;
and played among other tunes a simple little air ...

'But they didn't devote the whole evening to music. After a while
they played at forfeits; for it is good to be children sometimes, and
never better than at Christmas, when its mighty Founder was a
child himself. Stop! There was first a game at blindman's buff. Of
course there was. And I no more believe Topper was really blind
than I believe he had eyes in his boots. My opinion is, that it was a
done thing between him and Scrooge's nephew ...

London's best-known and oldest theatres, Covent Garden and *Theatres*
Drury Lane, were large buildings in which the audiences often
had to strain their ears to hear what was being said on stage. The
plays were nearly all five-act tragedies and comedies without
music (97).

> I gape in Covent Garden's walls,
> I doze in Drury Lane;

I strive in the Lyceum's stalls
To keep awake in vain.
There's naught in the dramatic way
That I can quite abide,
Except the pieces that they play
Upon the Surrey side.

Dickens was a regular visitor to the theatre and music hall and, like Leigh, who wrote this verse, he enjoyed the 'minor' theatres which were on the Surrey side of the Thames. These specialised in popular middle class melodramas such as *The Wandering Jew*, *Slaves of Barbary* and *White Maiden of California*.

At Astley's, one of these, the shows were often enlivened with performing horses, acrobats and sword fights: 'Dear, dear, what a place it looked, that Astley's! With all the paint, gilding and looking-glass, the vague smell of horses suggestive of coming wonders, the clean white sawdust down in the circus, the company coming in and taking their places, the fiddlers looking carelessly up at them while they tuned their instruments, as if they didn't want the play to begin, and knew it all beforehand! What a glow was that which burst upon them all, when that long, clear, brilliant row of lights came slowly up; and what the feverish excitement when the little bell rang and the music began in full earnest ... Then the play itself! The horses, the firing ... the forlorn lady ... the tyrant ... the man who sung the song with the lady's maid and danced the chorus ... the pony who reared up on his hind legs when he saw the murderer ... the clown who ventured on such familiarities with the military man in boots ... the lady who jumped over the nine and twenty ribbons and came down safe upon the horse's back— everything was delightful, splendid and surprising (98).' This description is by Dickens.

Heckling   Actors had to put up with a good deal of noisy heckling from the audience, as at a performance of *Hamlet* attended by Pip: 'Whenever that undecided Prince had to ask a question or state a doubt, the public helped him out with it. As for example; on the question whether 'twas nobler in the mind to suffer, some roared yes, and some no, and some inclining to both opinions said "toss up for it"; and quite a Debating Society arose. When he asked what should such fellows as he do crawling between earth and heaven, he was encouraged with loud cries of "Hear, hear!" When he appeared with his stocking disordered (its disorder expressed according to usage, by one very neat fold in the top, which I suppose to be always got up with a flat iron), a conversation took place in the gallery respecting the paleness of his leg, and whether it was occasioned by the turn the ghost had given him. On his taking the recorders— very like a little black flute that had just been played in the orchestra and handed out at the door—he was called upon unanimously for Rule Britannia (99).'

For those who could not afford to go to the theatre there were cheaper diversions like the 'penny gaffs' described by Henry Mayhew: 'In many of the thoroughfares of London there are shops which have been turned into a kind of temporary theatre (admission one penny), where dancing and singing take place every night. Rude pictures of the performers are arranged outside, to give the front a gaudy and attractive look, and at night-time coloured lamps and transparencies are displayed to draw an audience. These places are called by the costers "Penny Gaffs"; and on a Monday night as many as six performances will take place, each one having its two hundred visitors (100).'

'For a penny or less'

There were also peep-shows. An operator of one of these ex- plained to Mayhew: 'There are from six to eight scenes in each of the plays that I shows; and if the scenes are a bit short, why I puts in a couple of battle-scenes; or I makes up a pannerammer for 'em. The children *will* have so much for their money now. I charge a halfpenny for a hactive performance. There is characters and all— and I explains what they are supposed to be a-talking about ...

'The street-markets is the best of a Saturday night. I'm often obliged to take bottles instead of money, and they don't fetch more than threepence a dozen. Sometimes I take four dozen of bottles in a day. I lets 'em see a play for a bottle, and often two wants to see for one large bottle. The children is dreadful for cheapening things down. In the summer I goes out of London for a month at a stretch. In the country I works my battle-pieces. They're most pleased there with my Lord Nelson's death at the battle of Trafalgar. "That there is," I tell 'em, "a fine painting, representing Lord Nelson at the battle of Trafalgar." In the centre is Lord Nelson in his last dying moments, supported by Capt. Hardy and the chaplain. On

97

E

THE HAPPY FAMILY!

TRONIZED B MAJESTY

the left is the hexplosion of one of the enemy's ships by ours (101).'

The famous Fantoccini men toured the streets with their marion- *Fantoccini*
ettes. One described their programme to Mayhew: 'When we per- *marionettes*
form in the streets, we generally go through this programme. We
begins with a female hornpipe dancer; then there is a set of quadrilles
by some marionette figures, four females and no gentlemen. If
we did the men we should want assistance, for four is as much as
I can hold at once. It would require two men, and the street won't
pay for it. After this we introduces a representation of Mr Grimaldi
the clown,* who does tumbling and posturing, and a comic dance,
and so forth, such as trying to catch a butterfly. Then comes the
enchanted Turk. He comes on in the costume of a Turk, and he
throws off his right and left arm, and then his legs, and they each
change into different figures, the arms and legs into two boys and
girls, a clergyman the head, and an old lady the body. That figure
was my own invention, and I could if I like turn him into a dozen
(102).'

As travel became a 'social characteristic' it provided many *Getting away*
themes for writers. 'One of the most prominent "social character- *from it all*
istics" of the present time is the growth and progress of pleasure
travelling among the people. The working classes of thirty or even
fifteen years ago did not know their own country. Very few travelled
for pleasure ...'

But from the 1850s, 'industrious men of the Midland Counties
whose forefathers never saw the sea that encircles these islands are
enabled to gain physical as well as mental enjoyment by a view of
its mighty waters. Already the working classes in Manchester,
Liverpool, Sheffield, Birmingham, the Potteries and the great
Iron districts between Glasgow and Airdrie, as well as other places,
have commenced laying by their weekly pence to form a fund for
visiting London during the Great Exhibition of 1851. Were it not
for cheap excursion trains this great source of amusement and
instruction would have been unobtainable and the Exhibition
would have lost one of its great attractions (103).'

William Thackeray writing in *Punch* (1847) noted the popularity *Brighton*
of Brighton, made famous by the Prince Regent: 'The crowd, sir,

*Joseph Grimaldi (1779–1837) was a famous clown who entertained audiences in
London and the provinces for many years.

Facing page Some of the many street traders and entertainers who plied
their wares in the cities, *top left* broom seller, *top right* bird seller, *bottom
left* poultryman, *bottom right* pieman

on the Cliff was perfectly frightful. It is my belief nobody goes abroad any more. Everybody is at Brighton. I met three hundred at least of our acquaintances in the course of a quarter of an hour, and before we could reach Brunswick Square, I met dandies, City men, Members of Parliament. I met my tailor walking with his wife, with a geranium blooming in his wretched button hole, as if money wasn't tight in the City and everybody had paid him everything everybody owed him. I turned and sickened at the sight of that man.'

But was it really such fun being a tourist?:

> The last of the Londoners lagging behind,
> At this ruralising season,
> Retorts on the Tourists or rest of mankind,
> And boasts he has excellent reason.
>
> While they're on the strain in bus, steamer, and train,
> Through the land of JEAN PAUL or BÉRANGER,
> And are losing their luggage and temper in vain,
> He's not at such pains *se déranger*.
>
> While they're on a hunt for a bedroom to spare,
> Or for sheets—to be had for the spinning—
> He can have every bedroom in Bloomsbury Square,
> And acres of family linen.
>
> If coastwards they go, why the coast has its woes—
> Its landladies, artful old dodgers,
> With other unnameable pests of repose,
> Who break their long fasts upon lodgers ...
>
> In short, if for quiet and comfort you pant
> At breakfast, tea, dinner, and supper;
> Cut the country and come up to Town, if you want
> To throw off dark care from your crupper.

This verse was published in *Punch* (104).

The seaside The thrill of sea-side living is expressed in another verse published in *Punch* (105):

> I'm afloat, I'm afloat, what matters it where?
> So the devils don't know my address, I don't care.
> Of London I'm sick, I've come down to the sea,
> And let who will make up next week's number for me!

Ay my lodgins, I know, I'm done frightfully brown,
And e'en lobsters and shrimps cost me more than in town;
I've B.flats in my bed, and my landlady stern,
Says from London I've brought 'em to give her a turn.
Yet I'm happier far in my dear sea-side home,
Than the QUEEN on Dee Side, or Art-traveller in Rome;
A Cab-horse at grass would be nothing to me,
On the broad of my back floating free, floating free!

Seaside resorts like Blackpool, Hastings, Ramsgate, Southport *Bathing*
and Torquay were little more than fishing ports before the holiday *machines*
boom of the nineteenth century. One of their major attractions
for visitors was the opportunity to bathe. Although bathing huts or
machines were wheeled into the sea at some resorts, enabling bathers
to make a discreet entry into the water, there were complaints about
visitors who swam naked or wore revealing costumes.

Regulations for bathers were introduced by many towns and it
became a common practice for men and women to be segregated
on the beaches. A writer in *The Observer* (1856) described a beach
scene at Ramsgate: 'The beach where the machines are placed
from ten till one or two o'clock is so crowded with ladies and
gentlemen that it is difficult to walk through the throng, especially
if it be nearly high water. The visitors are close to the machines.
The water is black with bathers: should the sea be rather rough
the females do not venture beyond the surf, and lay themselves
on their backs, waiting for the coming waves ... The waves come,
and, in the majority of instances, not only cover the fair bathers,
but literally carry their dresses up their neck, so that, as far as
decency is concerned, they might as well be without any dresses
at all ... And all this takes place in the presence of thousands
of spectators ... In fact, it is looked upon much as a scene at a play
would be, as the gentlemen are there with their opera glasses ...

'If the gentlemen come to look at the ladies bathing, it is equally
the fact that ladies pay as much attention to the performances of
the gentlemen. The portion of the beach allotted to the men is
crowded with well-dressed females ... who calmly look on without
a blush or even a giggle ... How is it that ladies who are so very
delicate in London, should, when they arrive at Ramsgate, throw

101

UNDER THE CLIFFS · ON THE FORT

ON THE SANDS

off all pretensions to modesty and decency, as they do with their shawls and wrappers?'

By the 1860s many books had appeared which were specially *Books for* written for children. Boys could enjoy the adventure stories of *children* Captain Marryat, Mayne Reid and R. M. Ballantyne, or school stories like *Tom Brown's Schooldays* and *Eric, or Little by Little*. For girls the range was more limited, lying between fairy tales and stories about family life: *The Daisy Chain* (1856) by Charlotte M. Yonge was a popular example of the latter. About this time, two of the most successful children's stories were published—these were *Alice's Adventures in Wonderland* (1865) and *The Water Babies* (1863).

Fairy tales were popular too. They offered an escape into *Fairy tales* dreamland, far away from the noise and soot of industrial life: 'The fairies dance no more. Some say it was the hum of schools— some think it was the din of factories that frightened them; but nobody has been known to have seen them for many a year, except, it is said, one Hans Christian Andersen, in Denmark (106).'

Perhaps this is why Charles Kingsley's *Water Babies* (1863), too, was so popular. If the book was a fairy-tale, its language was surprisingly strong and true-to-life: '[The water-babies are] all the little children whom the good fairies take to, because their cruel mothers and fathers will not; all who are untaught and brought up heathens, and all who come to grief by ill-usage or ignorance or neglect; all the little children who are overlaid, or given gin when they are young, or are let to drink out of hot kettles, or to fall into the fire; all the little children in alleys and courts and tumbledown cottages who die by fever, and cholera, and scarlatina ...

There was a great vogue for nonsense stories and verse, often written in ballad form. Some thought it satirical, but whatever it was, it was best-selling entertainment:

'Tis the voice of the Lobster; I heard him declare,
'You have baked me too brown, I must sugar my hair.'
As a duck with its eyelids, so he with his nose
Trims his belt and his buttons, and turns out his toes.
When the sands are all dry, he is gay as a lark,
And will talk in contemptuous tones of the Shark:

Facing page Holidaymakers at Margate in 1872

But, when the tide rises and sharks are around,
His voice has a timid and tremulous sound.

(Lewis Carroll, *Alice in Wonderland*, 1865.)

If some Victorian entertainment seems over-romantic and indulgent to the modern world, we should not perhaps be surprised. The world they lived in, especially in the towns, was a dark one. Those who suffered from appalling social conditions might be excused a little self-pity.

In Dickens' time, many children's books were written to instruct as well as to entertain, and even in the most popular stories, a strong moral tone is apparent. We shall see some examples of this in the next chapter.

9 Religion and Science

THE EDITOR of one of the large number of magazines which were published for the young, told his readers: 'Our aim is to enthral you by wild and wonderful, but healthy fiction ... Our tales and articles do not contain "sermons in disguise" (107).'

However, many of those who wrote for children, like Dean Farrar, never missed a chance to preach at their readers:

> *We are not worst at once; the course of evil*
> *Begins so slowly and from such slight source*
> *An infant's hand might stop the breach with clay;*
> *But let the stream grow wider, and Philosophy—*
> *Aye, and Religion too—may strive in vain*
> *To stem the headlong current! ...*

Good and evil struggled fiercely in all the most popular stories of the time. Contemporary attitudes are vividly shown in this extract from Dean Farrar's best-seller, *Eric, or Little by Little* (1858):

'"You don't call that swearing, do you? ... I didn't swear, I only called that fellow a surly devil."

'"Oh, hush, Eric, hush," said Russell sadly. "You wouldn't have said so half a year ago."

'Eric knew what he meant. The image of his father and mother rose before him as they sat far away in their lonely Indian home, thinking of him, praying for him, centring all their hopes in him. In him! and he knew how many things he was daily doing and saying which would cut them to the heart. He knew that all his moral consciousness was fast vanishing, and leaving him a bad and reckless boy.'

105

E *

Nursery rhymes, especially, contained moral messages for the instruction of infants. Here is an example from Eliza Cook's *Poems* (1866):

A mouse found a beautiful piece of plum-cake,
The richest and sweetest that mortal could make;
'Twas heavy with citron and fragrant with spice,
And covered with sugar all sparkling as ice ...

He nibbled, and nibbled, and panted, but still
He kept gulping it down till he made himself ill;
Yet he swallowed it all, and 'tis easy to guess,
He was soon so unwell that he groaned with distress ...

'Ah me!' cried the doctor, 'advice is too late,
You must die before long, so prepare for your fate;
If you had but divided the cake with your brothers,
'Twould have done you no harm, and been good for the others ...'

Now all little people the lesson may take,
And *some* large ones may learn from the mouse and the cake;
Not to be over-selfish with what we may gain;
Or the best of our pleasures may turn into pain.

Peter Parley   Another 'message' was conveyed by Peter Parley in *Inquisitive Jack and His Aunt Mary* (1847): 'Although I profess to deal in matters that may amuse my young friends, I have a constant desire that, while they are entertained, they shall be instructed ...

'Our good Father in heaven, whom we all ought to love and obey, did not intend us to be savages; but he has provided only one way to avoid it, and that is by education ...

'A little chicken, only a day old, will run about and pick up seeds, which lie scattered among the stones and dirt. How does the chicken know that seeds are made to eat, and that stones are not made to eat? ...

'God has taught it—God has given it a wonderful instinct, by which it is guided in the choice and discovery of its food ...

'While instinct is the guide of the animal world, education is the instrument by which children are to reach their true destiny. God meant us to be educated; and children who hate education, hate God's will and God's way.'

106   The development of elementary education (see p. 53) owed much

to the efforts of religious bodies like the National Society and the *Religious differences* British and Foreign Society which, by the mid-century, had been joined by the Wesleyan Committee and the Catholic Poor School Committee. Progress towards a system of universal, compulsory schooling, however, would certainly have been faster but for the bitterness existing amongst the various denominations:

Victorians believed that it was their Christian duty to help the *Religious influence* less fortunate members of society—though this did not necessarily mean political reform. They gave their support to voluntary organisations which carried out a wide range of social work. In addition to education, this included the establishment of missions, orphanages, hospitals, and homes for the aged, as well as giving assistance to ex-prisoners, soldiers, sailors and young workers.

In a paper which he wrote on the subject of charity, Samuel Gurney reported: 'London is the headquarters of agencies which are at work throughout the country. Here the central bodies deal with the funds remitted from charitable residents in all parts of the United Kingdom. These are raised by bringing the objects of each society under the notice of the benevolent by personal canvass, by circular, or by public advertisement; occasionally by public dinners and fancy fairs; or in the case of missionary societies by a comprehensive system of local associations. The central executive consists usually of unpaid and paid officers, the unpaid being a president, treasurer, committee, and perhaps an honorary secretary, the paid being secretary, collectors and other subordinate officers. Generally the president is a nobleman or gentleman of influence (108).'

Although religion was a powerful influence in the lives of many *Non-churchgoers* people, there were others to whom church-going held little attraction. In 1853 Parliament obtained a Report on religious worship:

'The most important fact which this investigation as to attendance (at Religious Worship) brings before us is, unquestionably, the alarming number of non-attendants. Even in the least unfavourable aspect of the figures just presented, and assuming (as no doubt is right) that the 5,288,294 absent every Sunday are not always the same individuals, it must be apparent that a sadly formidable portion of the English people are habitual neglectors of the public ordinances of religion. Nor is it difficult to indicate to what particular class of the community this portion in the main belongs.

'The middle classes have augmented rather than diminished that devotional sentiment and strictness of attention to religious services by which, for several centuries, they have so eminently been distinguished. With the upper classes, too, the subject of religion has obtained of late a marked degree of notice, and a regular church-attendance is now ranked amongst the recognised proprieties ...

'It is to satisfy the wants of these two classes that the number of religious structures has of late years so increased. But while the *labouring* myriads of our country have been multiplying with our multiplied material prosperity, it cannot, it is feared, be stated that a corresponding increase has occurred in the attendance of this class in our religious edifices.

'More especially in cities and large towns it is observable how absolutely insignificant a portion of the congregations is composed of artisans. They fill, perhaps, in youth, our National, British, and Sunday Schools, and there receive the elements of a religious education; but, no sooner do they mingle in the active world of labour than, subjected to the constant action of opposing influences, they soon become as utter strangers to religious ordinances as the people of a heathen country.'

Dickens and the Church   Charles Dickens himself believed in a Christian God, but had little time for clergymen and disliked many of the practices of organised religion. He expressed his feelings in this passage from *Little Dorrit* (1857):

'It was a Sunday evening in London, gloomy, close and stale. Maddening church bells of all degrees of dissonance, sharp and flat, cracked and clear, fast and slow, made the brick-and-mortar echoes hideous ... Mr Arthur Clennam sat in the window of the coffee-house on Ludgate Hill, counting one of the neighbouring bells ... "Thank Heaven!" said Clennam, when the hour struck, and the bell stopped. But its sounds had revived a long train of miserable Sundays, and the procession would not stop with the bell, but continued to march on. "Heaven forgive me," said he, "and those who trained me. How I have hated this day!"

'There was the dreary Sunday of his childhood, when he sat with his hands before him, scared out of his senses by a horrible tract which commenced business with the poor child by asking him in its title, why he was going to Perdition? ... and which, for the further attraction of his infant mind, had a parenthesis in every other line with some such hiccuping reference as 2.Ep. Thess. c. iii. v. 6 & 7.

'There was the sleepy Sunday of his boyhood, when, like a military deserter, he was marched to chapel by a picquet of teachers three times a day, morally handcuffed to another boy ... There was the interminable Sunday of his nonage; when his mother, stern of face and unrelenting of heart, would sit all day behind a bible ... as if it, of all books! were a fortification against sweetness of temper, natural affection, and gentle intercourse. There was the resentful Sunday of a little later, when he sat glowering and glooming through the tardy length of the day, with a sullen sense of injury in his heart, and no more real knowledge of the beneficent history of the New Testament, than if he had been bred among idolaters. There were a legion of Sundays, all days of unserviceable bitterness and mortification, slowly passing before him.'

But the old religious order was about to face a crisis. When *Charles Darwin* published *The Origin of Species* in 1859, he seemed to be making a direct challenge to the teachings of the Church. The theory of evolution which he outlined was based on over twenty-five years' study of plants and animals. It suggested that new species were continuously appearing through a process of slow change. If the theory was correct, it meant that the Old Testament stories of the Creation and the Flood—which everyone believed—were untrue. Although Darwin's ideas came as a great shock, they did agree with other recent scientific discoveries, such as the unearthing of fossil remains of extinct mammals and reptiles. A great storm blew up.

On the 26 December 1859, *The Times* commented: 'The compass of science is practically illimitable. Hence it is that from time to time we are startled and perplexed by theories which have no parallel in the contracted moral world; for the generalisations of science sweep on in ever widening circles, and more aspiring flights, through a limitless creation, While astronomy, with its telescope, ranges beyond the known stars, and physiology, with its microscope, is subdividing infinite minutiae, we may expect that our historic centuries will be treated as inadequate counters in the history of the planet on which we are placed.

'We must expect new conceptions of the nature and relations of

its denizens, as science acquires the materials for fresh generalisations; nor have we occasion for alarm if a highly advanced knowledge, like that of the eminent Naturalist before us, confronts us with an hypothesis as vast as it is novel.

'This hypothesis may or may not be sustainable hereafter; it may give way to something else, and higher science may reverse what science has here built up with so much skill and patience, but its sufficiency must be tried by the tests of science alone, if we are to maintain our position as the heirs of Bacon and the acquitters of Galileo. We must weigh this hypothesis strictly in the controversy which is coming, by the only tests which are appropriate, and by no others whatsoever.

'The hypothesis to which we point, and of which the present work of Mr Darwin is but the preliminary outline, may be stated in his own language as follows: "Species originated by means of natural selection, or through the preservation of the favoured races in the struggle for life."'

And Charles Darwin himself wrote in *The Origin of Species* (1859): 'Let it be borne in mind how infinitely complex and close-fitting are the mutual relations of all organic beings to each other and to their physical conditions of life. Can it, then, be thought improbable, seeing that variations useful to man have undoubtedly occurred, that other variations useful in some way to each being in the great and complex battle of life, should sometimes occur in the course of thousands of generations?

'Origin of Species'

'If such do occur,' Darwin went on, 'can we doubt (remembering that many more individuals are born than can possibly survive) that individuals having any advantage, however slight, over others, would have the best chance of surviving and of procreating their kind? On the other hand, we may feel sure that any variations in the least degree injurious would be rigidly destroyed. This preservation of favourable variations and the rejection of injurious variations, I call Natural Selection. Variations neither useful nor injurious would not be affected by natural selection, and would be left a fluctuating element.'

In the years that Darwin was defending his advanced theories, ordinary people had their own mundane problems. For hundreds of years, people had been powerless to check the tragic effects of

War on disease

111

Facing page Charles Darwin, whose theory of evolution shocked many people

disease. It was still widely believed, in Darwin's time, that 'bad air' was the cause of typhoid, typhus and cholera. This view seemed to be supported by the fact that epidemics were more severe in towns than in the countryside.

But doctors were at last beginning to make some progress, and the authorities began to make serious studies of public health. An official report stated that:

'As a rule, the bread of London is made in what in houses in general is the coalhole and the front kitchen, the back kitchen being the place where the small store of flour is kept together with the other things in daily use ...

'The principal fact, for which I was not prepared, was their extreme dirt, and in many places the almost total covering of the entire space between the rafters with masses of cobwebs, weighed down with the flour dust that had accumulated upon them, and hanging in strips just above your head. A heavy tread or a blow upon the floor above, brought down large fragments of them ...

'Animals in considerable numbers crawled in and out of and upon the troughs where the bread was made ... the air of those small bakehouses is generally overloaded with foul gases from the drains.

'If slaughterhouses are inspected and subjected to regulations on sanitary grounds, there is quite as much reason, not only on sanitary grounds, but for the satisfaction of the public, in such an important matter as that of the making of their daily bread, that bakehouses should be dealt with on a similar principle (109).'

Cholera widespread

John Snow suggested that cholera was spread, not by bad air, but by the filth and sewage which littered the streets in those areas where the poor lived. But as the rich also became infected: '... there must be a way open for it to extend itself more widely, and to reach the well-to-do classes of the community. I allude to the mixture of cholera evacuations (*i.e.* sewage) with the water used for drinking and culinary purposes, either by permeating the ground and getting into wells, or by running along the channels and sewers into the rivers from which entire towns are sometimes supplied with water (110).'

Safer surgery

In the middle years of the nineteenth century surgery, too, became a more scientific occupation. In 1847 the Scottish physician, James Simpson, announced that he had successfully used chloroform during an operation. Though the introduction of anaesthetics was an important step forward, surgical operations continued to be extremely dangerous. It seems that about half of those who underwent surgery died. The main cause was the infection of gangrene.

Joseph Lister maintained that gangrene resulted from germs entering the wound, and decided to combat these with carbolic *Joseph Lister* acid. He explained: 'The material which I have employed is carbolic acid, which appears to exercise a peculiarly destructive effect upon low forms of life and hence is the most powerful antiseptic with which we are at present acquainted ... In conducting the treatment, the first object must be the destruction of any septic germs which may have been introduced into the wound, either at the moment of the accident or during the time which has since elapsed. This is done by introducing the acid of full strength into all accessible recesses of the wound ...

'I have now under my care in the Glasgow Infirmary a boy who was admitted with compound fracture of the leg as late as eight and a half hours after the accident, in whom nevertheless all local inflammation was avoided by means of carbolic acid, and the bones were soundly united five weeks after his admission ...

'The next object to be kept in view is to guard against the spreading of decomposition into the wound. This part of the treatment has been greatly improved during the last few weeks. The method which I have hitherto published consisted in the application of a piece of lint dipped in the acid, overlapping the sound skin to some extent, and covered with a tin cap which was daily raised in order to touch the surface of the lint with the antiseptic. In all the many cases of this kind which have been treated by myself or my house surgeons, not a single failure has occurred ...

'I left behind me in Glasgow a boy, thirteen years of age, who between three or four weeks previously met with a most severe injury to the left arm, which he got entangled with a machine at a fair. There was a wound six inches long and three inches broad ... the lower fragment of the bone, which was broken high up, was protruding four and a half inches ... Without the assistance of the antiseptic treatment, I should certainly have thought of nothing else but amputation at the shoulder joint; but as the radial pulse could be felt, and the fingers had sensation, I did not hesitate to

113

try to save the limb, and adopted the plan of treatment above described ...

'The boy continued free from unfavourable symptoms, while the limb remained as it had been from the first, free from swelling, redness or pain. Before I left, the bone was becoming firm ... If the severest forms of wounds heal thus kindly under the antiseptic treatment, it is obvious that its application to operation wounds must be merely a matter of detail (111).'

Nursing:
a new
profession
During the nineteenth century many more hospitals were built, and many women and girls entered the growing profession of nursing. Florence Nightingale became interested in nursing at an early age. When the Crimean War broke out in 1854, she was made 'Superintendent of the Female Nursing Establishments of the English General Hospitals in Turkey'. Accompanied by a small band of women, most of whom had no nursing experience, she travelled to the Crimea where conditions at the military hospitals were appalling. For the rest of her life she struggled to rid nursing of its 'Mrs Gamps' and to make it into a trained profession. Mrs Gamp was a character of Dickens in *Martin Chuzzlewit* (1844):

'Mrs Gamp tapped at the door (of her patient), which was immediately opened by Mrs Prig, bonneted and shawled ...

'"Anythin' to tell afore you goes, my dear?" asked Mrs Gamp, setting her bundle down inside the door, and looking affectionately at her partner.

'"The pickled salmon," Mrs Prig replied, "is quite delicious. I can partick'ler recommend it. Don't have nothink to say to the cold meat, for it tastes of the stable. The drinks is all good."

'Mrs Gamp expressed herself much gratified.

'"The physic an them things is on the drawers and mankle-shelf," said Mrs Prig, cursorily. "He took his last slime draught at seven. The easy-chair an't soft enough. You'll want his piller."

'Mrs Gamp thanked her for these hints ... and strolled up to the bedside to take a look at the patient ...

'Mrs Gamp solaced herself with a pinch of snuff ... By degrees, a horrible remembrance of one branch of her calling took possession of the woman; and stooping down, she pinned his wandering arms against his sides, to see how he would look if laid out as a dead man ...

114

Facing page Florence Nightingale, whose work helped rid nursing of its 'Mrs Gamps'

'"Ah!" said Mrs Gamp, walking away from the bed, "he'd make a lovely corpse!"'

Florence Nightingale wrote in her *Notes on Hospitals* (1859): 'The first requirement of a hospital [is] that it should do the sick no harm.'

And in her *Notes on Nursing* (1860): 'If a patient is cold, if a patient is feverish, if a patient is faint, if he is sick after taking food, if he has a bed-sore, it is generally the fault not of the disease, but of the nursing.

'I use the word nursing for want of a better. It has been limited to signify little more than the administration of medicines and the application of poultices. It ought to signify the proper use of fresh air, light, warmth, cleanliness, quiet, and the proper selection and administration of diet—all at the least expense of vital power to the patient.

'It has been said and written scores of times, that every woman makes a good nurse. I believe, on the contrary, that the very elements of nursing are all but unknown.

'By this I do not mean that the nurse is always to blame. Bad sanitary, bad architectural, and bad administrative arrangements often make it impossible to nurse ...

'We have it, indeed, upon very high authority that there is some fear lest hospitals, as they have been hitherto, may not have generally increased, rather than diminished, the rate of mortality— especially of child mortality.'

There was more than an element of truth in what she said. But the real cause of hospital mortality was still medical ignorance, not only in the classification of diseases, but about the nature of infection, and about the possibilities of anaesthetics. Real medical progress still lay in the future.

10 Towards Reform

DURING the 1850s a new kind of trade union came into being— that made up of skilled men in the same craft. Many earlier unions had ruined themselves by taking strike action without having sufficient funds, but the 'new model' unions, like the Amalgamated Society of Carpenters and Joiners, were less militant and concentrated their efforts on providing tangible benefits for their members.

A Government Commission praised them for throwing their energies into this direction: 'Without disguising from ourselves the shocking character of certain atrocities which have been clearly brought home to unionists in various parts of the country ... it is some satisfaction to feel that a very great improvement in the general character of unionism is shown as contrasted with the results of earlier Inquiries ...

'No question can exist in any mind that the best types of union are to be found in the older, richer, and best established societies. The general organisation, for instance, of the Amalgamated Society of Engineers, must strike everyone as a thoroughly efficient and complete system. As a mere administrative machine, it appears quite the equal of a high-class trading company ... The same thing might be said of ... the Amalgamated Carpenters, of the Manchester House Painters, of the miners', the glassworkers', the shipwrights', the printers', and many other societies of great extent and influence (112).'

These were some of the benefits a union member received: 'Does the 1*s* per week entitle a man to all the benefits you have specified? —a shilling per week and 3*d* per quarter to a benevolent and con-

tingent fund. The benefits are as follows: donation benefit for 12 weeks, 10s per week; and for another 12 weeks, 6s per week. For leaving employment satisfactory to branch or executive council, 15s per week; tool benefit to any amount of loss, or when a man has been a member for only six months, £5; sick benefit for 26 weeks, 12s per week, and then 6s per week so long as his illness continues; funeral benefit, £12 or £3 10s when a six months' member dies; accident benefit, £100; superannuation benefit for life, if a member 25 years, 8s per week; if a member 18 years, 7s per week; if a member for 12 years, 5s per week. The emigration benefit is £6, and there are benevolent grants, according to circumstances, in cases of distress (113).'

The first Trades Union Congress was held in 1868. G. Howell reports on the second, which was held in 1869. There was a large turn-out and wide-ranging agenda: 'The second of these congresses took place in the Odd Fellows' Hall, Birmingham, on August 23, 1869. The sitting of this, like the former one, lasted the entire week. Forty associations were represented, forty-eight delegates being present, representing 250,000 members ... The most prominent topic at each of these early congresses was the unprotected state of trade-union funds ... *Trades Union Congresses*

'In addition ... papers were read, and discussions arose, on piecework, hours of labour, the limitation of apprenticeship, the necessity for greater protection of the lives and limbs of those working in the mines, the objects and use of trade unions, strikes and lock-outs, conciliation and arbitration, co-operation and industrial partnership, national education, and ... the question of the direct representation of labour in Parliament (114).'

By the 1860s a further extension of the franchise could no longer be politically delayed. Gladstone, the Liberal leader, introduced a Reform Bill in 1866, but this was defeated. Robert Lowe, himself a Liberal, was amongst its most bitter opponents. The following year, with the Conservatives in power, a Reform Act was passed, the first Act of Parliamentary reform since 1832. It increased the electorate by a million and gave the vote to most urban male workers. *Parliamentary reform (1867)*

Mr Gladstone declared that since 1832, 'Parliament has been striving to make the working class progressively fitter and fitter for the franchise; and can anything be more unwise, not to say

119

more senseless, than to persevere from year to year in this plan, and then blindly to refuse to recognise its logical upshot—namely, the increased fitness of the working class for political power (115).'

Robert Lowe feared the consequences of such a policy: 'The working men of England, finding themselves in a full majority of the whole constituency, will awake to a full sense of their power (116).'

'The truth is,' said Lowe a year later, 'what was a conflict last year has become a race this year, and two parties are trying not which shall attack or which shall stand up for existing institutions, but which shall pass the other in attempting to reach first the goal of a perfectly level democracy (117).' The 1867 Act declared:

'*IV*. Every man shall, in and after the year, one thousand eight hundred and sixty-eight, be entitled to be registered as a voter, and when registered, to vote for a member or members to serve in parliament for a *borough*, who is qualified as follows [that is to say]:

1. Is of full age, and not subject to any legal incapacity, and

2. As a lodger has occupied in the same borough separately and as sole tenant for the twelve months preceding the last day of July in any year the same lodgings, such lodgings being part of one and the same dwelling house, and of a clear yearly value, if let unfurnished, of ten pounds or upwards; and

3. Has resided in such lodgings for the twelve months immediately preceding the last day of July, and has claimed to be registered as a voter at the next ensuing registration of voters ...

'*VI*. Every man shall, in and after the year, one thousand eight hundred and sixty-eight, be entitled to be registered as a voter, and, when registered, to vote for a member or members to serve in parliament for a *county*, who is qualified as follows [that is to say]:

1. Is of full age, and not subject to any legal incapacity, and

2. Is on the first day of July in any year, and has during the twelve months immediately preceding been, the occupier, as owner or tenant, of lands or tenements within the county of the rateable value of twenty pounds or upwards; and

3. Has during the time of such occupation been rated in respect to the premises so occupied by him to all rates (if any) made for the relief of the poor in respect of the said premises; and

4. Has on or before the twentieth day of July paid all poor rates

that have become payable by him in respect of the said premises up to the preceding fifth day of January.'

The 1867 Act was the most radical piece of political reform England had ever seen. There could be no going back now. The significance for the future was very great, and according to their lights men of all parties and beliefs could look forward to a new world of reform—not only inside Parliament, but outside too: in matters of public health, housing, conditions of employment, and union law.

Against the background of these momentous events, Dickens was writing what was to be his last novel, *The Mystery of Edwin Drood* (1870). The story was set in a town called Cloisterham, based on the real city of Rochester:

'An ancient city, Cloisterham, and no meet dwelling-place for 'Dickens dead' any one with hankerings after the noisy world. A monotonous, silent city, deriving an earthy flavour throughout from its Cathedral crypt, and so abounding in vestiges of monastic graves, that the Cloisterham children grow small salad in the dust of abbots and abbesses, and make dirt-pies of nuns and friars ... A drowsy city ... of another and bygone time ... The most abundant and the most agreeable evidences of progressing life in Cloisterham are the evidences of vegetable life in many gardens; even its drooping and despondent little theatre has its poor strip of garden.'

It was Rochester from where, many years before, the author had first despatched Mr Pickwick on his travels. The novel was planned for publication in twelve monthly parts, but it was never completed; only half appeared from April to September. Who was Dick Datchery? Was Edwin Drood really murdered? Dickens was not to answer these questions for, on 9 June 1870, he died at Gadshill, near Rochester.

His death was 'as if a personal bereavement had befallen everyone'. Dickens' first biographer wrote, 'The excitement and sorrow at his death are within the memory of all. Before the news of it even reached the remoter parts of England, it had been flashed across Europe; was known in the distant continents of India, Australia, and America; and not in English-speaking communities only, but in every country of the civilised earth, had awakened grief and sympathy. In his own land it was as if a personal bereavement had befallen everyone.

Queen's telegraph 'Her Majesty the Queen telegraphed from Balmoral "her deepest regret at the sad news of Charles Dickens's death"; and this was the sentiment alike of all classes of her people. There was not an English journal that did not give it touching and noble utterance; and *The Times* took the lead in suggesting that the only fit resting-place for the remains of a man so dear to England was the Abbey in which the most illustrious Englishmen are laid (118).'

Punch dedicated this poem to him on 18 June 1870:

CHARLES DICKENS dead! It is as if a light
In every English home were quenched today;
As if a face all knew had passed from sight,
A hand all loved to press were turned to clay.

Question who will his power, its range, its height,
His wisdom, insight,—this at least we know,
All in his love's warmth and his humour's light
Rejoiced and revelled,—old, young, high or low—

Learnèd, unlearnèd—from the boy at school
To the judge on the bench, none read but owned
The large heart o'er which the large brain held rule,
The fancy by whose side clear sense sat throned,

The observation that made all its own,
The shaping faculty that breathed life's breath
In types, all felt they knew and still had known,
Life-like, except that they are safe from death …

Mourn, England, for another great one gone
To join the great ones who have gone before—
And put a universal mourning on,
Where'er sea breaks on English-speaking shore.

His works survive him, and his works' work too—
Of love and kindness and good will to men,
Hate of the wrong, and reverence of the true,
And war on all that shuns truth's eagle-ken.

Further Reading

BOOKS BY DICKENS

1836–7	*Sketches by Boz*
1837	*The Pickwick Papers*
1838	*Oliver Twist*
1839	*Nicholas Nickleby*
1840	*The Old Curiosity Shop*
1842	*American Notes*
1843	*A Christmas Carol*
1844	*Martin Chuzzlewit*
1845	*The Chimes*
1846	*The Cricket on the Hearth*
	Pictures from Italy
1848	*Dombey and Son*
1850	*David Copperfield*
1853	*Bleak House*
	A Child's History of England
1854	*Hard Times*
1857	*Little Dorrit*
1859	*A Tale of Two Cities*
1862	*Great Expectations*
1865	*Our Mutual Friend*
1870	*The Mystery of Edwin Drood* (unfinished)

Charles Dickens also wrote many short stories and articles for a large number of journals and newspapers. For a time he was editor of *Household Words* and *All The Year Round*, in which journals his writings regularly appeared. He was the first editor of *Daily News*, a forerunner of cheap newspapers.

ABOUT DICKENS

Collins, P., *Dickens and Crime* (Macmillan).
— *Dickens and Education* (Macmillan).
Hardwick, M. & M., *The Charles Dickens Companion* (John Murray). This includes a biography, summaries of the novels, a who's who of the main characters and pages of quotations.
Hibbert, C., *The Making of Charles Dickens* (Longmans). An account of Dickens's early life.

BACKGROUND HISTORIES

Cruikshank, R.J., *Charles Dickens and Early Victorian England* (Pitman). Dealing mainly with the social scene.
Trevelyan, G.M., *Illustrated English Social History*, Vol. IV (Longmans).
Young, G.M. (ed.), *Early Victorian England, 1830–1865*, 2 vols (OUP). A detailed study, but more difficult than the above works.

BOOKS ON SPECIAL SUBJECTS

Hern, A., *The Seaside Holiday* (Cresset). A lively account of a topic which is little dealt with in most social histories.
Mayhew, H., *London Labour and the London Poor*.
Purves, G.D., *Mudlarks and Ragged Schools* (Humphrey). A short description of Lord Shaftesbury's work.
Rooke, P., *The Growth of the Social Services* (Rupert Hart-Davis). Has chapters on education, labour conditions, health, housing, etc.
The Great Exhibition 1851: A Commemorative Album (HMSO).

NOVELS

Disraeli, B., *Sybil*
Gaskell, E., *Mary Barton*
Hughes, T., *Tom Brown's Schooldays*
Kingsley, C., *Alton Locke*
— *The Water Babies*.

MISCELLANEOUS

Copies of contemporary journals such as *Punch*, the *Illustrated London News* and *Household Words* give authentic background material.

Notes on Sources

(1) Charles Dickens, *David Copperfield*, 1850
(2) Charles Dickens, *Little Dorrit*, 1857
(3) Charles Dickens, *David Copperfield*
(4) The Reform Act, 1832
(5) Parliamentary Report, Select Committee on Bribery at Elections, 1835
(6) Charles Dickens, *Nicholas Nickleby*, 1839
(7) Charles Dickens, *Pickwick Papers*, 1837
(8) Charles Dickens, *Our Mutual Friend*, 1865
(9) Charles Dickens, *Household Words*, 1853
(10) Charles Dickens, *Sketches by Boz*, 1836
(11) *Ibid*
(12) G. K. Chesterton, *The Pickwick Papers*, Everyman edition, 1907
(13) Charles Dickens, *The Pickwick Papers*
(14) *Ibid*
(15) Prince Albert, letter to Florschutz, 1837
(16) Prince Albert, letter to Baron Stockmar, October 1839
(17) *Punch*, 1843
(18) Benjamin Disraeli, *Sybil*, 1845
(19) Charles Dickens, *Hard Times*, 1854
(20) Royal Commission on the Poor Laws, 1834
(21) *Second Annual Report*, Poor Law Commission, 1836
(22) Charles Dickens, *Our Mutual Friend*
(23) Henry Mayhew, *London Labour and the London Poor*, 1851
(24) *Ibid*
(25) R. G. Gammage, *History of the Chartist Movement*, 1854
(26) Thomas Carlyle, *Chartism*, 1834
(27) Charles Kingsley, *Alton Locke*, 1849
(28) Chartist Petition to Parliament, 1838
(29) Select Committee on Public Petitions, *Hansard*, 1848
(30) Ebenezer Elliott, *Corn Law Rhymes*, 1831
(31) Richard Cobden, speech after the formation of the Anti-Corn Law League, 1838
(32) Disraeli, speech on the Third Reading of the Bill for the Repeal of the Corn Laws, 1846
(33) Frederick Engels, *Condition of the Working Class in England in 1844*
(34) Edwin Chadwick, *Sanitary Condition of the Labouring Population*, 1842
(35) Charles Dickens, *Hard Times*
(36) *Fourth Report*, Poor Law Commissioners, 1838
(37) Chadwick, *Sanitary Condition of the Labouring Population*
(38) Peter Gaskell, *Manufacturing Population of England*, 1833
(39) Frederick Engels, *Condition of the Working Class in England*
(40) James Leach, *Stubborn Facts from the Factories by a Manchester Operative*, 1844
(41) Leon Faucher, *Manchester in 1844*
(42) Commissioners on the Employment of Children in Factories, 1833
(43) Leonard Horner, *Parliamentary Papers*, 1837
(44) Children's Employment Commission, *First Report on Mines*, 1842
(45) Children's Employment Commission, *Second Report on Trades and Manufactures*, 1843
(46) Children's Employment Commission, *Second Report*
(47) Ashley in a Parliamentary speech, *Hansard*, 1846
(48) Ashley, *Hansard*
(49) Ashley, *Hansard*
(50) Charles Dickens, *Daily News*, 4 February 1846
(51) Charles Dickens, letter to Miss Burdett-Coutts, 12 August 1850
(52) Committee of Council on Education, 1843–4
(53) Select Committee on the Education of the Poorer Classes, 1838
(54) Rev. Tinling, *Minutes*, Committee of

Council on Education, 1847–8
(55) J. Fletcher, *Ibid*, 1843–4
(56) Rev. Allen, *Ibid*, 1846
(57) Rev. Bellairs, *Ibid*, 1843–4
(58) *Ibid*, August 1846
(59) *Newcastle*, Commission on the State of Popular Education, 1861
(60) The Schoolmaster, in *All the Year Round*, ed. C. Dickens, 28 May 1859
(61) Thomas Wyse, *Education Reform*, 1837
(62) Clarendon Commission on Public Schools, 1864
(63) Charles Dickens, *The Mystery of Edwin Drood*, 1870
(64) William Thackeray, *Vanity Fair*, 1847
(65) Charles Dickens, *The Old Curiosity Shop*, 1840–1
(66) Charles Dickens, *David Copperfield*
(67) Charles Dickens, *Nicholas Nickleby*
(68) H. Mayhew and J. Binny, *Criminal Prisons of London*, 1862
(69) *First Report*, Prison Inspectorate, 1836
(70) W. H. Dixon, *London Prisons*, 1850
(71) Charles Dickens, *Oliver Twist*, 1838
(72) Charles Dickens, *David Copperfield*
(73) Charles Dickens, *Daily News*, 13 March 1846
(74) Charles Dickens, letter to *The Times*, 14 November 1849
(75) *Reformatory Schools for the Children of the Perishing and Dangerous Classes and Juvenile Offenders*, 1851
(76) Mary Carpenter, *Reformatory Schools*, 1851
(77) Conference on Reformatory Schools, Birmingham, 1851
(78) Mary Carpenter, *Reformatory Schools*
(79) Charles Dickens, *Sketches by Boz*, 1837
(80) Petition of Mail Coach Contractors, Stage Coach Proprietors, and Postmasters and Innkeepers, upon or adjacent to the Great North Road between London and Edinburgh, 1838

(81) John Ruskin, *The Seven Lamps of Architecture*, 1849
(82) Select Committee on Railways, *Report*, 1844
(83) John Francis, *A History of the English Railway*, 1851
(84) Select Committee on Railway and Canal Amalgamation, 1852–3
(85) Thomas Hughes, *Tom Brown's Schooldays*, 1857
(86) James Caird, *English Agriculture in 1850–1*, 1852
(87) *Ibid*
(88) *Official Guide to the Great Exhibition*, 1851
(89) *Times*, 25 June 1850
(90) *Second Report of the Commissioners of the Exhibition*, 1852
(91) Edward Sullivan, in *The Nineteenth Century*, August 1881
(92) Charles Dickens, *American Notes*, 1842
(93) Charles Dickens, *The Old Curiosity Shop*
(94) Charles Dickens, *Household Words*
(95) *Punch*, 17 July 1858
(96) *Punch*, 21 August 1858
(97) H. S. Leigh, *Carols of Cockayne*, 1874
(98) Charles Dickens, *The Old Curiosity Shop*
(99) Charles Dickens, *Great Expectations*, 1862
(100) Henry Mayhew, *London Labour and the London Poor*
(101) *Ibid*
(102) *Ibid*
(103) *Illustrated London News*, 21 September 1850
(104) *Punch*, 19 September 1857
(105) *Punch*, 25 September 1858
(106) Frances Browne, *Granny's Wonderful Chair and its Tales of Fairy Times*, 1857
(107) *The Boys of England*, 1866
(108) Samuel Gurney, *Charitable Societies of London*, paper read to the International Philanthropic Conference, 1882

(109) H. Seymour Tremenheere, *Report* to the Secretary of State, Home Department, 1862

(110) John Snow, *On the Mode of Communication of Cholera*, 1855

(111) Joseph Lister, in the *British Medical Journal*, 1867

(112) Trades Union Commission, *Final Report*, 1869

(113) Trades Union Commission, *First Report*, 1867

(114) G. Howell, *Conflicts of Capital and Labour*, 1878

(115) William Ewart Gladstone, speech in the House of Commons, 12 April 1866

(116) Robert Lowe, speech in the House of Commons, 13 March 1866

(117) Robert Lowe, speech in the House of Commons, 5 March 1867

(118) John Forster, *Life of Charles Dickens*, 1872–4

Picture Credits

Index